PITTSBURGH IN WORLD WAR I

PITTSBURGH IN WORLD WAR I

ARSENAL OF THE ALLIES

ELIZABETH WILLIAMS

FOREWORD BY DR. JOSEPH F. RISHEL

Charleston · London

THE
History
PRESS

Published by The History Press
Charleston, SC 29403
www.historypress.net

Copyright © 2013 by Elizabeth Williams
All rights reserved

First published 2013

Manufactured in the United States

ISBN 978.1.60949.823.8

Library of Congress CIP data applied for.

For Mom and Dad

CONTENTS

FOREWORD

On June 28, 1914, the spark that ignited the European war occurred when Austrian archduke Franz Ferdinand and his wife, Sophie, were assassinated. By August, every major power had declared war except the United States. Sitting President Woodrow R. Wilson urged neutrality, and for the next two and a half years, the Americans steered an uncertain course in a vain attempt to avoid war.

Neutrality was not possible for a number of reasons, not the least of which was the fact that the United States was a nation of immigrants, most of whom held either loyalty or antipathy toward one of the two warring sides: the Allies and the Central powers. These loyalties were manifestly evident in industrial Pittsburgh, a city that had long been a magnet for European immigrants seeking a better life through employment in its many mills and factories. Pittsburgh's industrial area spread beyond the city limits along the three rivers of Allegheny County. According to the census of 1910, Pittsburgh, the eighth-largest city in the United States, had a population of 534,000, and the county had a population of just over 1 million. Of this latter number, 271,000 were foreign born, and another 342,000 were children of the foreign born. Thus, more than half the county's residents were first- or second-generation immigrants.

The Scotch Irish, no longer a new immigrant group and forming the backbone of the Pittsburgh elite, were adamantly in favor of Great Britain and France, chief among the Allies. The city's large German population, some of whom were more recent arrivals, supported two German language newspapers in greater Pittsburgh. These papers were outspoken on behalf of the fatherland and opposed any American involvement in the war on behalf of the Allies. Practically every East European ethnic group had a sizable presence in the area population. Among these most recent arrivals were Russians, Lithuanians, Poles, Czechs, Slovaks, Ruthenians, Ukrainians, Hungarians, Slovenes, Croatians, Serbians, Romanians, Bulgarians and Greeks. Many of these groups were reluctant supporters of their ancestral homelands because most of them had been trapped within the Russian or Austro-Hungarian Empires. In addition to them were large populations of Italians, Irish and English, the last of whom were hardly seen as "foreigners" at all. While Italians and English supported their home countries, the Irish, owing to centuries of oppression, had no love of England and supported the Central powers.

Economics played a huge role in the attitude of Pittsburghers and the nation at large. Hardly had the war begun than orders for ammunition and military equipment flowed into Pittsburgh-area companies. From the beginning of the war in 1914 to American entry into the war in 1917, some 250 Pittsburgh-area war plants grew to employ 500,000 men and women in nonstop production. It was the opportunity for full-time work that made the various ethnic groups suppress their differences, at least superficially, and work together. Ironically, many of those supporting Germany were employed making war material almost exclusively for the Allies' side.

Thirty-two long months were to pass before the United States entered the war. The 1915 sinking of the British passenger ship *Lusitania* made America's neutrality stance more difficult. By the time Wilson was up for reelection in 1916, the nation was deeply divided. Wilson won, but barely, with his opponent, Charles Evans Hughes, carrying Pennsylvania by a margin of fourteen percentage points. Hughes also carried Allegheny County. Wilson got few votes in Pittsburgh's German neighborhoods, such as Troy Hill or Arlington. Finally, unrestricted German submarine warfare, even on noncombatants, made it impossible to remain neutral, or at least it did in the minds of Wilson and Congress. On April 6, 1917, Congress declared war.

Pittsburgh enthusiastically contributed material to the nation's war effort. Local lore claimed that 80 percent of the army's ammunition came from Pittsburgh. The city and the surrounding area produced half of all the steel used by the Allies. Additionally, the city's factories produced prodigious amounts of guns of every size and description, armored plate, naval propulsion equipment, electrical machinery, railroad apparatus, electric motors and a plethora of other hardware. In the last year of the war, 1918, the men in the surrounding coalfields produced twenty million more tons than they had in the previous year.

The vastly increased demand for war production opened doors to women in areas of employment that had previously been closed to them. Although still denied entrance into "heavy" work occupations, women were widely recruited for work in ammunition factories. Westinghouse Electric organized a special bureaucracy to handle the influx of the female workforce. Their efforts included designing a special uniform for the women.

Of enormous help to the nation's war effort were the numerous inventions and organizational advances originating in Pittsburgh. Some of the first gas masks on the western front were developed at the Mellon Institute. Scientists, again at Mellon Institute, developed a standard aviation gasoline that gave Allies' airplanes a 20 percent increase in power. Pittsburgh-area firms developed ways to make munitions faster. They also developed stronger steel plate for tanks to resist machine-gun bullets.

Other innovations were organizational. Both Germany and the Allies had adopted daylight saving time in order to save fuel. The first convention for considering the measure in the United States was held in Pittsburgh on December 5, 1916. It endorsed the idea, and Congress enacted national daylight saving time in March 1918.

As Pittsburgh's industries girded for war, its young men answered the call either as volunteers or draftees. The adjutant general of Pennsylvania estimated that about 60,000 from Allegheny County entered the service. Of this number, a total of 1,527 soldiers and sailors were lost from all causes. In that newest of battlefields, the air, Pittsburgh sent over 500 men to become aviators, more than any other city, save New York. These men tended to come from the ranks of the socially prominent. Darling of the local newspapers was the intrepid aviator William Thaw II of the famed Pittsburgh business family. He is believed to be the first American to engage in aerial combat in World War I. His plane was shot down repeatedly, but each time, he managed to land safely behind Allied lines. Quite remarkably, Thaw lived through the war.

Thousands of other Pittsburgh men earned a less glorious war record, but they were heroes to the folks back home nonetheless. Women could volunteer for military service not only as nurses, as in wars past, but also as clerks, stenographers and telephone operators. Like women in other cities across the nation, Pittsburgh women had the opportunity to join the Woman's Land Army of America. They worked on farms, replacing men who had been called up for military service. Sometimes called farmerettes, they numbered about twenty thousand nationwide. Mothers of Democracy originated in Pittsburgh in the spring of 1918. It consisted of women who wished to keep in touch with men at the front and to assist them in maintaining communications with their loved ones back home. Mrs. Taylor Allderdice, of a locally prominent family, was the first president.

The American Red Cross in Pittsburgh was in a moribund state until February 1917, when a local chapter was reorganized. With American entry into the war, the Pittsburgh chapter sprung into action. On June 17, 1917, former president William Taft came to Pittsburgh to raise funds on behalf of the Red Cross. The total raised exceeded all expectations. By December, membership soared to 130,000, the largest of any city in the country. The Red Cross sent workers and countless tons of medical supplies to the troops. It also dispensed relief to Pittsburgh families of men in the service who were suffering sickness or poverty, and it operated canteen services to troops passing through Pittsburgh.

The war could not be paid for through current taxation; money had to be borrowed from a patriotic citizenry motivated to buy Liberty Bonds. As the war raged on, the federal government launched five separate drives. Each city was assigned quotas it was expected to fill through bond purchases. Pittsburgh exceeded its quota in all five drives. A total of $507 million was expected; instead, the city's residents reached into their pockets for a staggering $625 million.

Politically active Czechs and Slovaks thrust Pittsburgh onto the European diplomatic scene by negotiating the "Pittsburgh Agreement." Paving the way for the creation of the independent nation of Czechoslovakia, the agreement was signed by a group of twenty-nine Czechs and Slovaks in Pittsburgh on May 31, 1918. The primary author of the agreement, Tomas G. Masaryk, was elected the first president in November.

Late in the summer of 1918, as the war was drawing to a close, a catastrophe began that took many more lives than were ever lost on the battlefield through the entire war. A deadly influenza virus spread around the world in a pandemic, killing between 50 and 100 million people. It struck suddenly. Not wanting to disrupt the war effort, Pennsylvania health officials initially downplayed the disease but reversed themselves almost immediately. On October 4, 1918, the state health commissioner closed bars and theaters. The following day, Pittsburgh was under quarantine. The Catholic bishop of Pittsburgh at the time, Regis Canevin, closed all diocesan schools and churches. As fast as it struck, the influenza departed. In November, the quarantine was lifted. When it was over, the gruesome figures revealed that 5,340 Pittsburghers died of the influenza in the last four months of 1918.

As the pandemic was coming to an end, so was the war. Pittsburgh and the nation rejoiced when the armistice was signed on November 11, 1918. Their joy was tempered with a resolve not to forget those who served and those who gave the ultimate sacrifice. In remembrance of these heroes to the nation, some twenty-three tablets, ten statues and ten monuments were erected around the city. Nor did Pittsburgh neglect the international significance of the conflict. In 1921, the city dedicated its newest highway, on which tens of thousands still travel every day, as "the Boulevard of the Allies." It was a lasting tribute to America's sister democracies in a war that changed Pittsburgh's place in the world forever.

Joseph F. Rishel
Professor Emeritus
History Department
Duquesne University

ACKNOWLEDGEMENTS

It's certainly been an amazing year for me between wedding planning and writing this book. I'd like to give a big thank-you to everyone who helped me with the writing process. My entire extended family has been wonderful. I could not have done it without all of their love and support. I'd especially like to thank my wonderful husband, Andy Herrman; my parents, John and Roseanne Williams; and my brother, Andrew. My parents also provided me with a huge amount of help editing the book. Andrew and my cousin James Taggart helped me by taking many of the modern photographs that you see throughout this book. My aunt and uncle Janet and Raymond Luczak, as well as my cousin Charles Roof, also helped me by proofreading the book.

Outside of my family, so many others took time to help me with various aspects of this book. Dr. Joseph Rishel provided me with an amazing foreword. Karin Dillon, Katie McCurdy-Marks, Joseph Marks, Erin Murray, Dr. Susan Todhunter, Kimberly Watcher, Justinia White and Thomas White all provided editorial assistance.

Many people helped me gather materials for this book. Dr. Michael Shaussany provided me with images and took time to answer my questions. Many archivist and curators were kind enough to open their archives to me, including Ken White, the archivist at the Diocese of Pittsburgh; Donn Neal, the archivist at the Smithfield United Church of Christ; and Michael Kraus, the curator of Soldiers and Sailors. Art Lauterback and the staff at the Heinz History Center were also kind enough to assist me in locating images for this book. Greater Beneficial Union employee Julia Gaita provided me with information about the company's history.

The entire staff at the John J. Wright Library—Jackie Bolte, LaVerne Collins, Patti Dunn, Caroline Horgan, Marilyn McHugh, Darlene Veghts and Sister Agnes Vogel—has been extremely supportive during the last few months of the writing process.

I'd also like to thank Hannah Cassilly and the staff at The History Press for taking a chance on me and accepting my book for publication.

Lastly, I'd like to thank my teachers, especially Janet Aland, Jeff Flohr, Giovanni Puppo, Cindy McNulty, Dr. Edward Brett, Dr. Joshua Forrest and Dr. Paul LeBlanc, for pushing me to reach my fullest potential.

INTRODUCTION

Near the end of his life, Otto von Bismark, the chancellor of Germany responsible for German unification, predicted, "One day the great European war will come out of some...foolish thing in the Balkans." He died in 1898, sixteen years before his worst fears could be realized. On June 28, 1914, the heir to the Austro-Hungarian Empire, Archduke Franz Ferdinand, and his wife, Sophie, were gunned down in Sarajevo, Hungary, by Serbian nationalists. Due to a complex set of alliances between the major European powers, the continent was at war less than six weeks after the archduke's death. The United States declared its neutrality; the American public overwhelmingly wanted to stay out of what was seen as strictly a European conflict.

However, within one year, American sentiments began to shift when the British passenger liner *Lusitania* was sunk on its way from New York City to Liverpool, England, by a German U-boat, killing Americans. This was the first of many such attacks, which were followed by a litany of German apologies. Before America entered the war, seventeen American ships, as well as many foreign ones, had fallen victims to German torpedoes, killing over two hundred Americans, twenty-four of them children. By 1917, Germany had declared an all-out war on all commercial ships heading toward Great Britain. Realizing this would drive the United States closer to entering the war, Germany offered Mexico an alliance. In the telegram, Germany promised Mexico Texas, Arizona and New Mexico if it would ally itself with the Central powers and mediate between Germany and Japan.

The British intercepted and decoded the message, releasing what became known as the Zimmerman Telegram. This drastically drove public opinion in favor of war. The 1919 commemoration book *Pittsburg's Part in the World War: Souvenir Book* describes the feelings of many Americans: "The heel of the Hun despotism was to be set on Columbia's neck, on yours and mine. Our homes were to be as desolate as Belgium's have been."

By March 31, 1917, the United States had severed ties with Germany, and America's entrance into the war seemed inevitable. That night at eight o'clock, Pittsburghers gathered at the Pittsburgh Exposition Music Hall. The *Pittsburg Press* estimates that ten thousand people attended the meeting. There were too many for the hall to fit, so Pittsburgh mayor Joseph G. Armstrong ordered an overflow meeting be held on Duquesne Way, near the Point Bridge.

If there was any doubt as to the reason for the meeting, soldiers of every war as well as young, enlisted men, whose service would be necessary, marching shoulder to shoulder into the hall should have put that to rest. The principal speaker of the night was United States senator Philander C. Knox. He reminded those assembled of Germany's crimes against the United States while stressing that he did not know what actions President Wilson was going to decide in retaliation. He also reminded the audience that, no matter what was decided, "the United States has never engaged in a war of conquest. We have never unsheathed the sword except to protect and ensure our existence, to defend the honor of our flag, or to vindicate the principles of human liberty." He made it clear that he felt that if America entered into Europe's war, that statement would still hold true. Knox urged preparedness no matter what the outcome.

At the same meeting, Dr. Maitland Alexander, the pastor of the First Presbyterian Church, did not mince words when he spoke of the possibility of war: "We turn our eyes tonight across the seas and we behold the price that nations pay for war. Price in money…death, poverty, pain, and grief. It would be idle for us this evening to forget what war may mean to us. In our state of unpreparedness…With our vast cosmopolitan population, with disloyalty within and jealously without, with our lethargy begotten of our prosperity and our fat indifference born of our half-century of peace…But there are times when a man for principle, or home, or country ceases to count the cost. When he realized that the hour for words…is past." At the end of the night, those gathered proved that they took what was said to heart. In one voice, they swore a loyalty pledge: "I, recognizing clearly that the cherished ideals of liberty and justice in this country and the moral foundations of life itself are threatened with destruction by foreign enemies, do, voluntarily, and wholeheartedly, offer to the president and the government of the United States my loyal support in this coming crisis." Many of them had already proven their dedication to the war effort. Enrollment for the Red Cross had swelled so much that day that the *Pittsburg Press* dubbed it "Red Cross Day."

Two days later, on April 2, 1917, President Woodrow Wilson addressed the United States Congress in a speech that proved to be a defining moment for an entire generation of Americans. He urged Congress to abandon neutrality and enter into Europe's Great War, concluding, "To such a task we can dedicate our lives and our fortunes. Everything that we are and everything that we have, with the pride of those who know that the day has come when America is privileged to spend her blood and her might for the principles that gave her birth and happiness and the peace, which she has treasured. God helping her, she can do no other." In Wilson's mind, much like in Knox's speech a few days before, the war was a clear-cut battle of good versus evil, freedom versus barbarism. This moral absolutism was something that is characteristic of America throughout the war. In every major newspaper, and on many government posters, the Germans were reduced to nothing more than Huns, barbarians akin to Attila.

Pittsburgh, a city of immigrants, many of them German, had been contributing to the Allies' cause since the start of the war. In fact, in 1914, the first orders for steel and iron came in from Great Britain. It was during the First World War that Pittsburgh would claim the title "Arsenal of the World." Pittsburgh was at the very least the arsenal of the Allies. Half of all the steel used by the Allies was made in Pittsburgh.

Pittsburgh gave more than steel to the war effort. It also gave men. William Thaw of the first American aviators and Thomas Enright, one of the first American casualties, were born and raised in the Steel City. Pittsburgh women also flocked to the front lines as nurses. Pittsburgh's Red Cross branch was one of the largest in the country. The citizens of Pittsburgh also bought Liberty Bonds in record numbers. It was a city that was filled with intense patriotism, but under that patriotism, there was a great deal of fear, tension and division.

In this book, I intend to give you a sense of what Pittsburgh was like during the Great War. Pittsburgh was, when America entered the war, the nation's eighth-largest city. It was fundamental and critical to the Allied war effort. The war and America's involvement in it, in turn, defined a generation of Pittsburghers. Yet this history is often overshadowed by that of the Second World War. It is my intent to shed some light onto this important

Downtown Pittsburgh, 1914. *Courtesy of the Heinz History Center.*

Artist's depiction of Fifth Avenue at Smithfield Street at night around 1916. *Author's Collection.*

period in the city's history. This is by no means meant to be an exhaustive portrait, detailing every piece of the local scene. That would take several books much longer than this one. I will, however, examine several aspects of life in Pittsburgh during the war, such as Pittsburgh's various industries, Pittsburgh's German American community and the three major local colleges during the war (Duquesne University, the University of Pittsburgh and Carnegie Tech, now Carnegie Mellon University). Although several chapters of national charities, such as the Salvation Army, the YMCA and the YWCA, contributed a great deal to the war effort, my primary focus will be on the American Red Cross. A portion of my book will also be devoted to discussing some of the Pittsburghers who served in Europe. I hope you find this as fascinating a time in Pittsburgh's history as I do.

I will end my introduction with a grammatical note. You will notice that Pittsburgh will sometimes be spelled Pittsburg without the *h* throughout the course of the book. I have not misspelled it. Although in 1911 Pittsburgh had reclaimed the *h* at the end of its name, some local newspapers (such as the *Pittsburg Press*) and other contemporary sources that I will be quoting had not switched the spelling back as of 1917. For the sake of authenticity to my sources, whenever I reference or quote a source, I will spell it as they did. However, for the bulk of my text I will spell Pittsburgh properly.

CHAPTER ONE

CIVILIAN ORGANIZATIONS
IN PITTSBURGH

Clara Barton founded the American Red Cross, one of America's premiere humanitarian relief organizations, in May 1881. However, only a small Red Cross chapter existed in Pittsburgh in July 1916. The Pittsburgh Chapter did not really gain its footing until early April 1917. When President Wilson asked the United States Congress to come to Britain and France's aid and declare war on the Central powers, everything changed.

In Pittsburgh, the Red Cross was staffed by mostly well-meaning volunteers who had little experience and training. They just knew that Europe needed their help, and they were going to rise to the challenge. It was a hectic time, and the Pittsburgh Chapter could not expect much help from the national headquarters. All over the country local Red Cross chapters were going through the same growing pains, and the national headquarters was stretched very thin. In spite of the early difficulties, a temporary office was secured in Schenley High School (which had opened in September 1916), auxiliaries were formed and members poured in. In less than a month, the Pittsburgh Chapter of the Red Cross went from a small, disorganized group to a full-fledged organization ready to take on the new challenges the war presented.

By the end of April, the Pittsburgh Chapter had the largest membership in the United States, double that of New York City. Women formed the majority of these early recruits, and immigrants also joined in droves. In *The Pittsburgh Chapter of the American Red Cross*, authored by the Red Cross after the war, the organization explained, "They knew better than Americans what war meant. It was their own kin across the water who were dying on a hundred battlefields…They knew the great work of the Red Cross in alleviating the suffering throughout Europe; and when they enrolled in the Red Cross, it was not only in dedication, but in gratitude as well." For the immigrant population of Pittsburgh, especially those who had come from countries that were now the enemy, Red Cross work provided a way for them to prove their loyalty to America.

In November 1917, enrollment of nurses for war service began. Many of Pittsburgh's best and brightest nurses answered the call, and many ardent young women went to the Red Cross with the hopes of becoming field nurses. Reflecting after the war, the Red Cross was harsh when writing of these young recruits, describing them as "romantic young women who hardly had an idea of the serious business in which the nation was engaged. Their vague notions were rooted in generous impulses, but they were a sore trial to people who were bearing somewhat more than the loads, which were originally expected of them…All this time, the great hospitals in the city were short, as ever before, of nurses, and were eager to take any eligible young women for training." The authors are perhaps too harsh on these young volunteers. These young women were motivated by the same sense of patriotism and duty as their brothers and sweethearts were when they enlisted in the army. Young people of both sexes had romantic notions of war and the glory that came with it.

Some nurses were sent to training camps within the United States, but most were sent to France, most notably to the University of Pittsburgh's Base Hospital 27. (In addition to the Pittsburgh Red Cross, many other local nurses were sent there. Mercy Hospital alone sent thirty-eight women, as well as several male physicians.) Two Red Cross nurses died in France, and several nurses returned home injured and unable to work. The exodus of nurses to the war effort left a void in Pittsburgh that the Red Cross attempted to fulfill. The Educational Department set up classes for young women to become nurses' aids. This became particularly important with the influenza outbreak in the fall of 1918 when nurses left for other affected cities before the outbreak hit Pittsburgh, further exasperating Pittsburgh's nursing shortage. Before the war was over, fifty-two classes, each with 780 students, graduated from the program. These classes were open to women, both young and old, of all races and nationalities.

Another important piece of the Red Cross's work was the Women's Motor Corps. In the spring of 1917, 12 young women decided to learn how to drive in the event the Red Cross would need that skill. By July, they were

American Red Cross poster used to recruit Pittsburgh nurses to the Red Cross. *Courtesy of the Library of Congress.*

ready and willing to transport raw materials and supplies from the Red Cross headquarters to the various workrooms throughout the city. (This was not unique to Pittsburgh; Women's Motor Corps sprang up around the country.) The national headquarters required them to take special classes in sanitary troop drills, first aid and auto mechanics. The colonel in charge of the U.S. armory was tasked with their military training. As the Women's Motor Corps grew, those duties were later taken over by the captain in charge of the soldiers who were training at the Schenley Park Oval. The women wore regulation motor corps uniforms and had a structure similar to the military. Eventually, as the organization grew to nearly 200 women, there were 16 officers and 181 privates. Each company had a first and second lieutenant as well as two sergeants.

The cars that they drove were either their own or donated by private citizens. When the women realized that cars would not be sufficient for their needs, they raised money to buy their own trucks. At the height of the war, there were forty cars and seven trucks in service every day. From December 1, 1917, through January 1, 1920, the women donated 14,636 hours of service, hauled 1,342 tons of freight and transported 25,879 packages for the

Red Cross and other organizations, such as the United War Work Camp, the Liberty Loans Drive, the War Exposition, the New East Relief Campaigns and the Children's Welfare Bureau.

When the Women's Motor Corps was not called on to transport packages, it was transporting people. Members drove social workers all over the city, and during the flu epidemic, which hit Pittsburgh in October 1918, they transported doctors. When disaster struck, such as when a TNT plant exploded in Oakdale in May 1919 or when there was an explosion in a box factory on Bigelow Boulevard, the Women's Motor Corps rushed to the scene. The brave young women did everything from administering first aid and rushing victims to the hospital to transporting bodies to the morgue. When they were not otherwise engaged, they also acted as ambassadors to the city, giving tours to important visitors, such as the famous French soldiers known as the Blue Devils.

A major part of the efforts of the Pittsburgh Red Cross, especially near the beginning of the war, was fundraising. The first war fundraising campaign was announced in May 1917 and took place in June. The national headquarters told the Pittsburgh Chapter it was expected to raise $1 million, 75 percent of which was to go back to the national headquarters. That number was later raised to $3.5 million. The Pittsburgh fundraising campaign kicked off on June 11 with a dinner at the William Penn Hotel where ex-President William Howard Taft, honorary chairman of the American Red Cross, spoke. In attendance were ninety of Pittsburgh's most prominent men. Underneath each of the guests' plates was a slip of paper containing the dollar amount that the Red Cross believed each person, or the corporation he represented, could contribute. The Red Cross later reported that this tactic was successful. One by one, those who gathered silently opened their wallets. Although some attendants needed to clear it with their corporations' boards, everyone gave or pledged something. One man in particular, perhaps seeking to outdo the others with his philanthropic spirit, doubled his requested amount. Although this was an impressive showing of support, most of the money was raised by volunteers going door to door. They raised $3,952,732.18 in that particular campaign.

One of the first needs that the Red Cross sought to fill was sending supply kits and Front Line Packets for the army and navy. Supply kits included surgical dressing, hospital garments and knitted articles. Front Line Packets included various surgical dressings. The supply department, with its eight paid workers and hundreds of female volunteers, took the lead in filling the military's orders. From October 1, 1917, until after the armistice was signed, the workrooms were open Monday through Friday from 9:00 a.m. to 6:00

p.m. Occasionally, if there were large orders to fill, they would open earlier on Mondays and Fridays as well as on the weekends. At noon every day, the work would pause, and the women would have a moment of silent prayer.

Work in the supply department was anything but cheerful. They worked in silence; there was no talking or laughing allowed. Upon completion of an object, it then needed to be inspected to verify it met Red Cross standards. If it did not, the worker would have to redo it. Often standards or orders would change once a woman started working, and she would have to start over. The amount of completed goods that Pittsburgh was responsible for every month was issued to them from the national headquarters. As they worked, fear and uncertainty sometimes gripped the workroom. At various times throughout the duration of the war, rumors circulated that the raw materials for making the surgical dressing were being poisoned before they reached the Red Cross. As a result, all the materials were then sent to Pittsburgh Testing Laboratories to verify they were not sabotaged.

In addition to its other duties, the Red Cross was also responsible for making hospital garments. At first, when the garment orders were complete, the Red Cross required that each garment be washed before being sent outside the city. However, many of the women workers were well off and had never done laundry before. Servants were difficult to find, as many working-class women had left their jobs for the more lucrative millwork. Eventually, the Red Cross determined that in order to expedite things, the garments could be washed later.

Sweaters and socks were also knitted by Red Cross workers for the troops. While workers were expected to provide their own yarn, needles were provided by the Red Cross until January 1918. Demand for the sweaters was often greater than supply, and as a result, the Red Cross was placed in an embarrassing situation. Women who had been knitting for months believed the goods they had made had gone to family members on the front line. However, these women started receiving letters from their husbands or sons telling them that they were cold and had not received their sweaters. This was eventually corrected. The Red Cross made sure that local men were provided with sweaters before they shipped out. By February 1918, sweaters were distributed at the draft board headquarters.

In September 1918, the Pittsburgh Chapter of the Red Cross was asked to collect fruit pits and shells from nuts. Because of a coconut shortage, the government had trouble securing the type of carbon gas masks required. A replacement for this carbon was contained in pits of certain fruits and the shells of certain nuts. To make a single gas mask, they needed either two

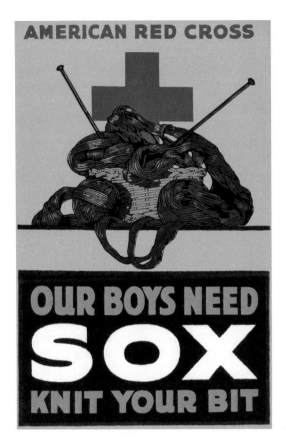

Left and opposite: National Red Cross posters used by the Pittsburgh Chapter to encourage Pittsburgh women to knit for the troops. *Courtesy of the American Red Cross.*

hundred peach pits or 7 pounds of shells. November 9, 1918, was designated Gas Mask Day. Receptacles and displays were sent to restaurants, bakeries, hotels and stores all over the city. After collection, the pits were dried and packed. Pittsburgh answered the call for shells and pits admirably. The Red Cross reports that 181,700 pounds of pits and shells were shipped from Pittsburgh. They were in the middle of packaging another shipment when the armistice was signed.

The Junior Red Cross was another important aspect of the Pittsburgh Chapter of the Red Cross's work during the war. It is also an excellent example of the fervent patriotism that was gripping the city. In August 1917, the principal of Schenley High School presented a plan to organize a Junior Red Cross facility in every school in the city. By Christmas, there were ninety thousand Junior Red Cross members. By June 1918, that number more than doubled. Nearly every school in the city, public and private, enrolled as an auxiliary. Schools became auxiliaries in two ways: either every student

contributed a quarter to the Red Cross or they would pledge to do certain types of volunteer work. Almost every school did both. The money was raised in a number of ways. Schools with students that could not afford the quarter held fundraisers where they sold items that the students made. Others had their students donate a penny a day.

The Red Cross sought to educate school children so they could, in turn, educate their parents. The students learned to respect the food regulations set out by the U.S. Food Administration. They learned how to conserve food at home and received war gardening tips. Teachers visited their students' homes to ensure the students and their parents knew what to do. Older children were also sent door to door to educate their neighbors.

In addition, the Junior Red Cross made itself useful in other ways. The boys made everything from refugee furniture and lamps to artificial limbs, canes, crutches and splints. The girls made clothing for refugees and hospital supplies. School gardens were also tended by students. The fresh vegetables were then used in the school cafeteria. Younger children were put to work making paper dolls for the children of war-torn countries overseas, along with scrapbooks and joke books for American troops. These books were small, bound by tape and often included magazine articles from before the war as well as various jokes and colorful pictures. They were small enough to be held in one hand, and thousands of them were used in hospitals overseas. High school students provided valuable assistance to both the Red Cross and the draft board in the form of clerical work. To keep morale high among the students, they would sing patriotic songs and the national anthems of the Allied nations, which were provided by the music departments of various high schools.

Perhaps one of the Red Cross's most vital services was to provide canteens to the troops, most notably those overseas, but they also provided relief for those passing through Pittsburgh from other parts of the country. In July 1917, Pittsburgh formed the Relief for Troops Committee, which greeted the incoming soldiers. The railroads reported to the Red Cross how many

Opposite, top: Some of Irwin Avenue High School's Junior Red Cross workers, May 1918. *Courtesy of the Heinz History Center.*

Opposite, bottom: Like children all over the country, students at Dilworth School worked in their school garden, September 7, 1917. *Courtesy of the Heinz History Center.*

troops to expect the next day, and workers would make care packages for the soldiers. Eventually, women, not men, were primarily responsible for greeting the trains. Unlike their male counterparts, though, they were not allowed to board. Instead, they handed the packages to the soldiers through the train windows, unless the officer in charge made his men get out and stand in formation. On hot days, in addition to the care packages, the women would often serve ice cream cones to the troops, and on cold days, they would serve coffee. From September 1917 until November 1919, these men and women served more than 680,000 American troops.

The Red Cross also provided traveling troops with an Information Station in the Pennsylvania Railway Station waiting room beginning in July 1918. It was staffed by Red Cross workers from 8:00 a.m. until 10:00 p.m. Meant to service men traveling in smaller units or alone during a stop over in Pittsburgh, it allowed soldiers to check bags, and it provided them with paper, stamps, postcards, matches and apples. Poor soldiers were given free meals. They also provided tickets to the local swimming pool for service men who wanted to swim. If a man wanted to see the city, a car was provided for him. Red Cross workers, if time allowed, would also take him to the theater or their homes to share a meal with the workers' families. By January 1919, this service was open twenty-four hours a day, seven days a week. Men worked all night to make sure the troops were provided with hot coffee and sandwiches. Eventually, the Red Cross opened two canteens, one at the Pennsylvania Railroad and one at the B&O Railroad. These rest stops contained a dining area, a drinking fountain, couches, desks and comfortable chairs.

Another important aspect of the Red Cross's work in Pittsburgh was home service and civilian relief. In April 1917, the Red Cross formed the Civilian Relief Committee and began to train social workers, under the direction of the University of Pittsburgh, to assist the families of soldiers who were overseas. Over one hundred people graduated from this program and went on to donate $10,000 worth of time and energy to the Red Cross.

The Red Cross also assisted the Appellant Board of Allegheny County District with appeals for exemption from service that the appellant board had refused. The Red Cross reviewed every case and made recommendations regarding draft exemption. This benefited the Red Cross because it gave the organization access to families that would need assistance. It also gave the draftees whose requests had been denied the peace of mind that the Red Cross would help their families. The Red Cross also assisted many immigrants whose knowledge of American laws and the English language was poor. They presented immigrants' cases to the appellant or draft board for them, and if the cases were denied, the Red Cross assured them that their families would be taken care of. The Pittsburgh Chapter of the Red Cross was one of the only chapters in the country that worked with the draft board in this way. It also tried to keep in touch with the men it helped as they mobilized.

The Red Cross helped soldiers' families by supplying medical services, clothes and bedding. It helped people secure employment. Sometimes, it would convince well-off family members to assume responsibility for their less fortunate kin. Other times, the Red Cross itself would provide aid in the form of loans. Because of the financial support to the families of soldiers, many children who would have otherwise left school to support their families were able to continue their educations. *The Pittsburgh Chapter of the American Red Cross* discusses one family, two parents and nine children, whose oldest son went to war. Shortly after he shipped out, his mother and his eight siblings contracted influenza. His father worked irregularly due to his health, and the family was in dire straights. The Red Cross nursed the family back to health. It also managed to persuade a daughter who had been estranged from the family to return. Once the father recovered, a son who was old enough to work was given training and employment was obtained. A daughter, who was born with a bone condition, received care that she would not have otherwise received, as well as vocational training. Another daughter wanted to quit school and go to work to help her family. The Red Cross provided financial assistance and persuaded her to remain in school. She received her diploma, graduating with highest honors.

When Pittsburgh doughboys came home from the war with severe wounds, the Red Cross was there to arrange for their care. For example, one man who came home paralyzed had lain injured in a shell hole for four days and was lucky to be alive. The Red Cross described him as a "mental and physical wreck." His family was unable to shoulder the burden of his care alone, so the Red Cross stepped in. Its doctors prescribed him a special diet, a wheelchair and other medical necessities. It also took care of his mental health. As his injuries had left him depressed, the organization provided him with outlets. He was given puzzles and games, and he was taught beadwork and the mandolin. When his strength returned and he saw the joy of living again, they arranged for him to learn a trade. He took training in Show Card Advertising and learned how to make cane chairs and baskets.

The Red Cross also provided bail to soldiers who, upon returning home, got into trouble with the law. After the war, it, along with various other charitable organizations, assisted returning soldiers in finding employment. Many uneducated veterans received vocational training through these programs.

The Mothers of Democracy marching in one of the many parades Pittsburgh held to drum up local support for the war. *Courtesy of the Heinz History Center.*

In addition to the services it provided the troops and their families, the Red Cross was also of great service to the local immigrant community. Many new Pittsburghers still had relatives in war-torn Europe. It was not possible for people to communicate with them, but the Red Cross, because it is an international relief organization, could. The only country whose citizens it could not get information about was Germany because Washington forbade it. This is not surprising, given the general suspicion of those with ties to Germany that was running rampant at that time.

In May 1918, membership in the Red Cross was restricted to those willing to recite an oath swearing to "defend the United States against all enemies, foreign and domestic." In Pittsburgh, only one potential Red Cross volunteer refused to recite the oath of allegiance and was not allowed to join. Most Pittsburghers who wanted to join the Red Cross had no problem with the oath, as many were undoubtedly also members of one of the dozens of ultra-patriotic organizations that had sprung up around the country and spread to Pittsburgh.

By the end of the war, over twenty thousand Pittsburgh families had received assistance from the Red Cross in one way or another. The Red Cross did work that was necessary in Pittsburgh, although it was not without help. Many Pittsburghers and Pittsburgh organizations rose to the challenge to help the Red Cross accomplish its work. A local association for the blind helped it care for wounded soldiers. The Boy Scouts helped with civilian relief work. Private companies also assisted. For example, an oil refining company offered petroleum for medical purposes. An electric company donated its services to provide power to the temporary headquarters. Another company donated all the rugs and blinds that it used. Private citizens offered uses of their cars; one donated $25,000 to the Base Hospital unit. Throughout the war, all the space that the Red Cross used was rent free.

Another organization that helped was the Mothers of Democracy, also called the Sisterhood of War Mothers or the Democracy Mothers, which was founded in Pittsburgh in 1918 and was the brainchild of Red Cross volunteer Ellen Allderdice. Its intention was to provide a different sort of relief to Pittsburghers. Although anyone was welcome to attend their meetings, the Mothers of Democracy were intended to be primarily an organization of American women who had sons serving in the military. Their goal was to promote pro-American feelings and provide comfort for one another during wartime. Their meetings were full of singing, dancing and speeches. Additionally, letters they received from their sons were often read, and soldiers home on leave were guests of honor. They also took part in parades as well as Liberty Loan drives. After the war, they cared for those who had not received their sons' back pay as well as those "orphaned" by the war. According to the *Gazette Times*, many war widows could not care for their young children or had to be institutionalized because of grief. The Mothers dedicated themselves to caring for these children. Mary McGuinness, chairman of the child welfare committee, proudly told the paper that the committee had convinced a well-off woman looking to adopt a dog to take a child instead.

CHAPTER TWO

THE ARSENAL OF THE WORLD

In 1868, Bostonian James Parton described Pittsburgh as "hell with the lid off." So much smoke and smog filled the air that white sheets hung out to dry quickly turned black. Andrew Carnegie wrote, "The smoke permeated and penetrated everything…If you washed your face and hands they were as dirty as ever in an hour. The soot gathered in the hair and irritated the skin, and for a time…life was more or less miserable." Smoke abatement measures were fundamentally opposed by industry because of the cost. Pittsburgh's smog contributed to the city having some of the highest morbidity and mortality rates in the nation for the first twenty or so years of the twentieth century. Lung diseases, such as pneumonia, were especially common and deadly. That was the high cost that Pittsburghers paid for the city's industries. The pay off was that Pittsburgh was the epicenter of a large industrial district (spanning from Lake Erie to the coal mines of West Virginia, encompassing many of the small towns in western Pennsylvania). It was also home to a variety of large companies such as Westinghouse, Pittsburgh Plate and Glass and Aluminum Company of America. Most of all though, there were the steel mills. It might have been known as the "Smoky City," but Pittsburgh was the king of steel by the outbreak of the Great War. In 1912, two years before the start of the war, it was already producing 36 percent of the total output of steel in the United States, which equaled 12 million tons.

Naturally, when war broke out in Europe, the Allied nations turned to Pittsburgh. Pittsburgh did not let them down. One general even remarked that "Pittsburgh steel is everywhere along the battlefront." The Allied troops shot Pittsburgh-made bullets out of guns made from Pittsburgh steel. They were protected by Pittsburgh barbed wire. They even used Pittsburgh gas masks to protect them from German gas. For a brief time, Pittsburgh was no longer just the "Smoky City" or "hell with the lid off." It became the arsenal of the world.

The Westinghouse Corporation gained the distinction of becoming the first American company to receive an Allied contract on December 30, 1914. The British government needed three million shells. There was only one problem: Westinghouse was not a munitions company. Despite this, it accepted the contract without having any idea how to fill it. To make a shell, 128 operations and fifty-one inspections were required. It also needed to use sixty-five gauges in inspections. Inspecting fusel caps was a 170-step procedure. Since only 2 percent of the tools the corporation had in the plant were able to be used to make shells, Westinghouse needed to first manufacture many of the necessary tools, as well as new machinery. Undaunted by the massive task facing it, it managed to complete the order in forty-five days.

Impressed with Westinghouse's work, the British government gave the company more and more orders, including manufacturing howitzer shells. In less than a month, Westinghouse had an entire plant dedicated to manufacturing these shells. Three months after the factory was built, it was producing 5,000 shells a day. Pittsburgh also made shells and freight car brake equipment for the Russian and French governments. By the end of the war, Westinghouse alone made 5,058,000 shells for the British army. The remainder of the Pittsburgh plants produced millions more bullets, shells and cartridge cases for the British navy. In addition to those, 200,000 cartridge cases were made for the Russian government in Pittsburgh.

Pittsburgh was a hotbed of creativity during the war. On April 22, 1915, Germany changed the way the war was fought by releasing the first deadly gas attack. At the time of the attack, Dr. James Garner, senior fellow in natural gas investigations at the Mellon Institute, was studying the recovery of sulphur dioxide from copper smelter gases. Garner and his team had discovered a wood charcoal that when specially prepared had absorbent powers for sulphur dioxide. The charcoal could also be reused. Garner and his assistant, Howard D. Clayton, realized that if they could design a mask, their charcoal treatment might be useful against German gas attacks. So, with the help of Dr. R.F. Bacon, the director of the Mellon Institute, they designed one of the first gas masks used in the war. Garner's wife constructed it.

After they had their prototype completed, they needed to test it. Garner, using press dispatches that described the gas as having a yellow and greenish tint, hypothesized that the Germans were using bromine and chlorine gases. So Clayton, in a move of incredible bravery, offered to risk his own life to test the mask. A window was opened in a room adjacent to Garner's lab and a cylinder of liquid chlorine was placed in it, leaking a fatal amount of gas. Clayton entered the room and sat there for over a half an hour before he even noticed the smell of the gas. The mask had been a success. Immediately, they told the British who requested at least twelve masks. Within two weeks, the British had Garner's gas masks in hand. While there is some debate over whether or not Garner's mask was the first type of gas mask used in the war, it was, at the very least one of the first.

Dr. A.C. Fieldner, the chief chemist at Allegheny County's station of the U.S. Bureau of Mines, developed the Tissot gas mask, which was primarily used by American troops. In April 1917, he began researching different substances that could sufficiently absorb the gas. Although he already knew that soda lime and charcoal would work, there were many different grades of each. He experimented by putting the absorbent into test tubes about six inches long and two inches wide (about the size of the canister contained in the gas mask) and passing a mixture of gas and air (as it would be on the battlefield) through it. He timed the gases' progress through the tube until he determined which combination of absorbents offered the most resistance. The first of these masks offered ten to eighteen hours of resistance, although Fieldner and his team managed to increase the amount of time to forty to fifty hours by the end of the war.

The first man to test the Tissot masks was Bureau of Mines consultant and Yale University School of Medicine professor Dr. Yandell Henderson. Although the mask protected his face and lungs, the gas bleached his hair and ruined his clothes. Between April and September 1917, twenty thousand gas masks were made in Pittsburgh and tested for service. In September, the American government decided to move the work on the Tissot masks to Washington. Fieldner was granted the rank of major in the U.S. Army and placed in charge of the work. After the war, Fieldner rejoined the Bureau of Mines and worked to adapt his gas mask for industrial use.

Dr. Martin A. Rosanoff and his students at the Mellon Institute also worked to develop a new type of homogenous gasoline for airplanes. In the summer of 1917, French aviators realized that the best type of gasoline contained ingredients of intermediate weight, nothing too light or too heavy. Rosanoff was interested immediately and was encouraged to study it at a conference in the fall of 1917. He immediately attempted to interest the army in his studies. However, the American government did not show an interest until the Signal Corps sent a telegram in March 1918, requesting preparation of some of his gasoline. The U.S. Bureau of Standards advocated Rosanoff's gasoline in July 1918, after discovering that it gave an advantage of 20 percent over the gasoline it had been using. The bureau said that it believed that Rosanoff's method was the only way that American airmen could gain an advantage over the Germans. The Signal Corps, in response, built the first plant, under Dr. Rosanoff's supervision and directions. His students were even granted exemptions from the draft, and mechanics were chosen from enlisted men to aid him.

While the Mellon Institute and Fieldner were working on saving lives, Westinghouse was developing more effective ways to take them. They invented a rifle grenade, which is a type of grenade that is launched from the barrel of a rifle, allowing it to travel farther than a hand-thrown one. Its rifle grenade was accepted by both the French and Italian governments, and over eight million were ordered. The company was expected to produce twenty-five thousand a day. To meet the demand, Westinghouse built a new plant. Within three months of the groundbreaking on the new plant, it was shipping eighty-eight thousand a day. By April 1917, when the United States entered the war, Pittsburgh was more than ready to meet its government's needs. It had 250 war plants, which were operational twenty-four hours a day, seven days a week. Around 500,000 Pittsburghers were already employed in war work.

When America entered the war, it too turned to Pittsburgh for its war materials. A national publication, the *Christian Science Monitor*, said in February 1918, "It is not merely an industrial city; it is a city of stupendous industries. It is a city of furnaces, of rolling mills, of foundries, a plate-making city; a huge arsenal upon which all the nations fighting for humanity, civilization and democracy are today drawing largely for their supplies. And Pittsburgh is one of the numerous things which the high command of Germany overlooked when it set the world on fire." By the time the war ended, Pittsburgh had produced 80 percent of all the munitions used by the American army. Nearly every plant and industrial center in the region was dedicated to the war effort. The numbers almost seemed surreal. For example, the Pittsburgh Plate and Glass Company produced sixty-five thousand pounds of optical glass, which went into gun sights. That was enough to supply the entire American army and navy. The Aluminum Company of America produced more 3 million tin cans for American army rations.

Westinghouse worker making a grenade. *Courtesy of the Library of Congress.*

Westinghouse was also responsible for building a ninety-thousand-horsepower turbine engine for the government, which at that time, was the largest ever built. Westinghouse engineers also developed a grenade launcher for the American Army, which ordered 529,655 of them. Each month, Westinghouse shipped thousands of carloads of fans, wireless telegrams, telephone instruments, portable dynamos (devices which could be hand cranked to provide an electric charge), feet warmers (used by men who were in the crow's-nest of ships) and numerous other types of electrical equipment.

Pittsburgh's mills made many different types of gun forgings, as well as heavy shells and ammunition. By the end of the war, the total tonnage it produced was five to ten times greater than any other industrial center. The Carnegie Steel Company was charged with making the larger artillery and produced over two thousand forgings between the 155-mm gun and the 240-mm howitzer, and no other plant in the world produced more. Pittsburgh

This poster was used to remind Pittsburghers of Carnegie Steel's support for American troops, 1917. *Author's Collection.*

engineers also developed a more efficient forging process, which the British and French adopted. Over 3.5 million shells were made in Pittsburgh just for the American forces. In August 1918, the U.S. government asked the Carbon Steel Company to develop a type of tank armor that would not be penetrated by machine gun fire fifty feet away. They asked that 700 be made by October. The company developed and manufactured Molybdenum Steel, testing it by firing at it with a machine gun mounted to the roof of their plant. By October, they more than filled the government's demands. They made a record-setting 725 sets of the armor in the time allowed.

As demand for munitions increased, the U.S. government purchased 130 acres of land on Neville Island (located in the Ohio River just south of downtown Pittsburgh) and entered into an agreement with United States Steel to build a munitions plant. It was designed to be the largest producer of guns and shells in the entire country, dedicated to producing the larger guns especially. The government also planned to develop 500 acres of the island for a town dedicated to the plant and its workers. They planned on building five to ten thousand houses to house upward of 100,000 people. The plant and the town were meant to be permanent fixtures on the island. Despite the fact that the government had already spent $12 million on the plant, it was abandoned after the armistice was signed.

World War I also led Westinghouse to develop one of the world's first commercial radio stations, KDKA. Westinghouse was involved in radio and broadcasting development for the British government, and by the time the American government entered the war, two experimental radio stations were active in Pittsburgh, one at a Westinghouse facility in East Pittsburgh and the other at a private home five miles away. When the armistice was signed, Westinghouse found itself with a large amount of time and money invested in radio equipment and searched for a way to make it profitable. H.P. Davis, the vice-president of Westinghouse, whose project was developing the radio broadcast, read a Pittsburgh newspaper, which carried an advertisement for a department store selling radio receivers in order to listen to Westinghouse's broadcasts. Davis took the idea and ran with it, thus KDKA was born in 1920.

The war also meant a great deal of revenue for the city of Pittsburgh. For example, on November 1, 1918, the American government had contracts in Pittsburgh totaling $214,405,000. By the end of the war, Westinghouse estimated that its contracts with all the Allied governments alone totaled $1,475,000,000.

Despite the massive output from Pittsburgh companies, there were delivery problems throughout the war. The factories quickly realized that they could make products quicker than the railroads could deliver them. As a result, there were constant traffic jams on railroads. Occasionally, plants had to shut down because, in addition to railroads not being able deliver finished products, they were sometimes unable to deliver the raw steel-producing materials, coke and coal, to the factories and mills. Pittsburgh was after all, producing more steel and products than ever before. Shipping and traveling by rivers also became an issue in the winter months when the rivers froze. In the summer, extreme heat and humidity would make the mills and furnaces nearly impossible to work in and sometimes disrupt their output. Because of the massive war orders, especially after the United States entered the war, it was often hard for nongovernmental entities to get steel. The *New York Times* reports that by May 1918, it was impossible for a new buyer to get steel unless it had connections inside the mills already or had special credentials issued by the government.

Accidents were not an uncommon occurrence. In February 1917, two thousand shells were destroyed by fire when the Union Switch and Signal Company's plant in Swissvale went up in flames. It was the company's largest plant dedicated to making switch signals in the United States. The fire, which started in the packing department, was reputedly caused by spontaneous combustion. The fire was so large and out of control that it took firefighters from four different boroughs as well as the city of Pittsburgh to extinguish it. It probably did not help that they were forced to stand idle for a half an hour because the water plugs were frozen. The fire caused $4 million in damage.

In early November 1918, shortly before the armistice was signed, twenty-eight men lost their lives, and twenty more were hospitalized due to a gas leak in one of the Jones and Laughlin plants. Although the gas feeding the furnace was off, the tank sprang a leak, asphyxiating more than forty men. It took rescue workers several hours to recover the men because they were hindered by the presence of gas.

The accidents and the death toll were all part of the darker side of Pittsburgh's industries. There was a fundamental fear among the big companies of Pittsburgh of their workers, especially their unionizing. United States Steel led the way to keep unions out of Pittsburgh. Its tactics ranged from giving frequent wage increases to fear and intimidation. Politicians, newspapers and churches were counted on to support management. In the towns outside the city, Pennsylvania's Coal and Iron Police worked with big steel to keep workers in line using unsavory tactics.

The immigrant labor force was huge and unassimilated. Immigrants spoke different languages. They held their own beliefs and customs, lived in their own communities and often had their own churches. They were seen as having little in the way of ties to the greater community. In short, however necessary they were, the immigrant labor force was the unknown, which is always terrifying (a theme that categorizes the war years, even outside industry). Many Americans saw them (especially Italians and Slavs) as predispositioned to have Leftist and anarchical sympathies even before the war. Also, in the war years, there were a large number of German immigrants employed in Pittsburgh's industries.

The fear of German sabotage and German immigrants was very real, particularly after the United States entered the war. Troops and extra guards were stationed at every factory producing war materials. Bridges were illuminated at night so that these guards could see anyone approaching. On April 8, 1917, the *New York Times*, speculated:

> *Some of the most important official and mechanical positions are held by unnaturalized Germans. Should a movement be started to intern these men, a great hardship will be suffered by the whole country. As long as they use no seditious methods and maintain the peace they will not be molested unless it becomes absolutely necessary for the safety of operations to place them under guard. In the past two years Germans employed at local munitions plants have earned from $8 to $12 a day making war materials to fight their own countrymen. Every industry in this great theatre of labor is honeycombed with them. Hence the question of how they will behave in this crisis has attracted attention. In most cases they have been taken aside and interrogated as to how their sympathy for their native land would lead them. In no instances is there any record of a German being discharged to date.*

The Germans of course were not interned in camps. Nor were they dismissed en masse. However, Pittsburgh's leading industries did employ a large network of spies in their workforce. The largest companies in Pittsburgh could afford to maintain their own "secret services". Others pooled their resources and engaged in what historian Charles McCormick describes as "industrial espionage cooperatives." The Employers' Association of Pittsburgh was one such cooperative, used by Mesta Machine Company, Westinghouse Air Brake, Union Switch and Signal and many others.

Several detective agencies were also active in and around Pittsburgh, encouraging the idea that the immigrant worker and labor unions were dangerous and offering their services to management. (During the war years, 1915–1919, over twenty agencies advertised in Pittsburgh newspapers.)

While the word *detective* might conjure the image of Arthur Conan Doyle's perpetual "good guy" Sherlock Holmes or former Pinkerton detective Dashiell Hammett's hard-boiled Sam Spade in the modern mind, it was a completely different story during the war. Detective was more likely to conjure up an image of, according to McCormick, a man who was, "shady, often boozy, sleazy, [a] liar or a publicity seeking incompetent." They were used as strikebreakers or to spy on workers.

While perhaps not as negative as public opinion, they sometimes resorted to violence (as the Pinkertons had during the Homestead Steel Strike in 1892). Overall, they were not on the side of the immigrant, the worker or the Radical Left. Generally, the detective was a lower middle–class American-born man who held a negative opinion of the immigrant population. Immigrants were generally viewed by lower middle–class nativists as a group to be suspicious of and a threat to their very way of life as well as future advancement. Added to that, the livelihood of these men often relied on worker-management conflicts. They were in no hurry to disprove the management's suspicions that its workforce and that workforce's desire to unionize was founded on a desire to become militant and radicalized. Detectives also inflated their own importance and often relied on hearsay as much (if not more) than direct evidence. However, they did need to strike a balance. Companies would not pay for services that did not produce accurate, cost-effective results. In order to keep the agencies and detectives honest and to ascertain they were getting their money's worth, companies would often hire multiple detectives who did not know each other to work on the same project. In effect, they hired spies to spy on their spies.

As for the Radical Left in Pittsburgh, it was one of the targets not only of big business but also of the federal government. While I am only going to give a small overview of the Radical Left and the government's surveillance of it here, a full account of it is provided in Charles McCormick's interesting and highly readable *Seeing Reds: Federal Surveillance of Radicals in the Pittsburgh Mill District, 1917–1921*. While the Radical Left in Pittsburgh was small and relatively tame in comparison to that of other cities (such as New York, Chicago and Cleveland), it still posed a threat in Pittsburgh. While the threat of revolution was remote, strikes and slowdowns would affect the industries' bottom lines. Unionizing the industrial workforce, which the Left sought to do, would only increase the threat of massive stoppages.

The Socialist Party of America (SPA) did have a presence in Pittsburgh and the surrounding areas that made up the Pittsburgh district, its power peaking between 1900 and 1917. By 1912, it had two thousand members in the city alone, and several prominent elected officials in Pittsburgh and the surrounding areas were socialists. The socialist party even had a Sunday section dedicated to its events in the *Pittsburg Press*. The Northside was home to Young People's Socialist League schools. Throughout the city, ethnic and social clubs housed foreign language branches. While some scholars contend that 1912 was the beginning of the SPA's decline in Pittsburgh, few people realized that when World War I broke out. It was a significant, growing political organization. It had several thousand sympathizers, and five hundred to one thousand activists. These men and women were predominantly immigrants, or first- and second-generation Americans, who were skilled workers or worked white collar jobs. Their goal was to slowly educate the masses so they would vote socialist and therefore defeat capitalism. Despite internal struggles (often based on regionalism: for example, the Hill District's socialist often clashed with Homestead's socialist), the SPA was the only political organization that was strong enough to oppose American participation in the war and oppose militarism. However, it was often ignored by the federal government in favor of the much more radical Industrial Workers of the World (IWW), which was seen as part of a secret conspiracy to agitate labor.

Although the IWW was exceptionally active nationally in the spring of 1917, it did not have much of a presence in Pittsburgh. In fact, the Bureau of Investigation (BI, a forerunner to the FBI) could not find a visible IWW group to place under surveillance until receiving a tip. The tipster, a socialist, said that there were 150 radicals and IWW members operating in secret within the city. The leaders of the group were placed under surveillance, and arrests were later made for distributing anticonscription propaganda. Radicals, like those in the IWW, even if they were American born, felt that immigrant workers were the key to their success. American-born workers were seen as too individualistic and too invested in the American Dream and the hope that their better-educated children could have a better life. This, of course, further identified radicalism with immigrants and increased nativist fears. When a strike did occur in Pittsburgh, it was often blamed on the Radical Left and immigrant workers.

By and large, industrial workers were among the highest paid in the city. For example, munitions workers at Westinghouse were paid between ten and twenty-six dollars a day during the war. Although that may not seem like much money by modern standards, when compared to the six dollars (plus expenses) a week that the BI special agent in charge Robert Simms Judge was making in 1915, it was considerable. However, for the industrial worker the hours were long and the working conditions were often unsafe, hot and dirty.

The war had caused a massive amount of orders for materials, but it also stopped immigration from Europe. The resulting labor shortage would be dealt with in a variety of ways by corporations (including the recruitment of African American men from the South discussed later in this chapter). It also led to conditions that were highly favorable to the workers. Workers around the country, ready to use the labor shortage to their advantages, were inclined to strike in order to demand better working conditions. In Pittsburgh, there were several small strikes, particularly in the early days of the war, which sometimes only affected one or two departments in a factory. Generally, these did not last long, but there are two strikes that I consider notable. The first began in late April 1916 at the Westinghouse plant in East Pittsburgh and eventually spread to include over thirty thousand strikers. This strike is notable not only for its size but also for its leaders. Many women took a leading role in the strike, as well as (to the derision of the Pittsburgh newspapers) many socialists who were unaffiliated with the company. One of the strike's primary leaders was Fred H. Merrick, editor of the socialist paper *Justice*. The other strike that I will discuss occurred in September 1917 at the Jones and Laughlin's Eliza Furnace. Although not as large as the 1916 strike, it occurred after America entered the war. As a result, the strikers faced charges of being un-American.

In April 1916, three weeks before 13,000 Westinghouse workers would strike, the company received signs of worker discontent. Westinghouse had been attempting to implement scientific management techniques with the goal of rationalizing its plants. This caused what the workers perceived to be an endless reorganization and added to the workers' grievances over long hours, piecework, job classification and pay structure. Mechanics, working in the W-5 section of the East Pittsburgh plant, went on strike, demanding a pay increase. Westinghouse quickly assented to their demands giving them a 10 percent pay increase and double overtime. Three weeks later, 1,800 men in W-5, along with thousands of other employees (including 2,300 to 3,000 women), decided to strike, demanding an eight-hour day and that their union be recognized by the company. On the first day of the strike, April 22 (Holy Saturday), hundreds of picketers surrounded the plant. They formed a human chain at three of the gates in an attempt to bar entrance for over 4,000 workers. Most workers entered through a gate leading from the Pennsylvania Railroad's private bridge, which led from the railroad station into the plant. As the bridge was owned by the railroad, picketers could not block it. (Throughout the duration of the strike, this bridge became known as the "scab bridge" by the picketers.)

Soon fights broke out between the workers trying to enter and the picketers. One man was recognized by the crowd as a detective and was driven away from the plant. After being chased for blocks, he finally admitted that he had been employed by an agency but had worked as a machinist at the plant for the past few months. Satisfied, the strikers beat him and sent him home.

Other men were so terrified that they dropped their lunches and ran (these lunches were later used to feed the picketers). Two men, Carol Semm and Conley Albrighton, were arrested for disorderly conduct. Both men were released with a ten-dollar fine. However, their arrest led to a standoff at the police station. Around 1:30 in the afternoon, six hundred picketers led by a "dish-pan drum corps" stormed the police station demanding the men's release and making it clear they would resort to force if necessary. When Police Chief Sode informed them they had been released, the crowd took control of the station and told the police chief that they would not tolerate interference. Sode responded by saying that he only had fifty men and that there was no way he could interfere with the strikers. He made it clear that Westinghouse was going to have to rely on paid guards to protect the plant. Satisfied, the leaders of the strike gave a speech on the steps of the station before they left.

For those who made it inside the factory, tension was high. The lunches of every man that the plant guards deemed suspicious looking was checked for bombs. Saloons were also closed until after the gates to the plant had closed out of fear that adding alcohol to the mix would make an already tense situation worse. Picketers remained through the night, succeeding in keeping many night workers who had left from returning to work.

Upon learning of the strike, other Pittsburgh companies weighed in on the eight-hour workday, and eighty-three said they would not decrease their employees' hours. This further aggravated the strikers as well as many other workers in Pittsburgh. Union Switch and Signal's opposition to the eight-hour workday would eventually lead workers at their Swissvale plant to join the striking Westinghouse workers.

On April 24, more trouble broke out at the East Pittsburgh plant. According to the *Pittsburg Press*, ten thousand picketers, including many women, blocked the entrance to the plant, again forming a human chain. A squad of deputy sheriffs attempted to break the chain, even using their clubs and maces on the strikers. They did manage to break it once; however, it quickly reformed, and the deputy sheriffs were attacked by the strikers. Railroad detectives had to drive forty strikers from the bridge so that workers could enter the plant. Despite this, the strikers were able to collect the pay that they earned for the first half of April. Fear of the violence that would break out if the strikers were allowed to use it to buy liquor kept the saloons closed until 7:00 p.m. and wholesale liquor dealers did not sell liquor over the counter. By the next day, the National Guard was preparing to enter the strike zone if it was needed. This put many of the guardsmen in an awkward situation, as several knew the strikers and many strikers were also in the National Guard.

Socialist and strike leader Fred H. Merrick was arrested on April 25. He was stopped on the Cable Avenue Bridge by Assistant Chief Deputy Matthews who asked him if he was a picketer. When Merrick answered that he was not, Matthews told him to move on. Merrick refused and was arrested. Although other strikers attempted to intervene, they were stopped. While Merrick was quickly released, he would eventually be sentenced to three and a half years in jail for his role in the strike, effectively removing him from the Pittsburgh scene for the duration of the war.

On April 26, ten thousand strikers marched on the Westinghouse Airbreak Plant in Wilmerding. While five thousand of the picketers were stationed at the plant's entrance, another five thousand were stationed at a tunnel leading to the plant. The picketers clashed with both police and detectives but managed to keep 2,000 of the plant's 3,500 workers out. While it is inevitable that some workers probably joined the picketers, others simply went home out of fear. Because of management fears that violence was inevitable if the plant continued to operate, it was shut down except for necessary personnel. The Shadyside Westinghouse plant also shut down. Despite its near closure, the threat of violence at the Airbreak plant remained. On April 27, thirty-five-year-old Louisa Johnbusky pushed her way through the crowd when what employees remained were leaving the plant for the day. She brandished a revolver and screamed "scab" at the men. She was quickly subdued and arrested, opting to spend ten days in jail rather than pay the ten-dollar fine.

To add to an already tense situation, the deputy sheriffs hired by Westinghouse to help control the situation were accused by Wilmerding's police department and firefighters of attempting to incite a riot. On April 28, the ten firefighters who had been helping the police keep order went back to the fire station, and the nine-member police department threatened to resign if the sheriffs were allowed to roam the streets. The firefighters believed that any riot started by the deputy sheriffs would be blamed on them, and the police agreed. They felt that there was very little trouble and that they could handle it on their own, and they considered it an insult to have the armed guards around town. After that, deputies were made to stay on Westinghouse property.

Westinghouse Airbrake Plant, around 1916. *Author's Collection.*

Opposite, top and bottom: Strikers march in Braddock, Pennsylvania, demanding an eight-hour workday during the 1916 Westinghouse Strike. The wooden fence surrounding the Edgar Thompson Works in Braddock is also depicted. *Courtesy of the Library of Congress.*

By May 1, thirty-six thousand workers had been brought out of their factories. As Pittsburgh's transit workers were also on strike, a general strike in the Pittsburgh district seemed inevitable. Recruiters from other industrial centers, like Detroit, flocked to Pittsburgh in an attempt to convince some of the now out-of-work men to come to their cities, promising them better hours and higher paying jobs.

Despite earlier talk of sending the National Guard in to quell the strike, the government did not want to intervene in a labor dispute. That changed when the strikers tried to draw out the workers at the United States Steel's Edgar Thompson Works in Braddock. The mostly unarmed strikers faced armed opposition. When a boy threw a stone into the yard, men came out of the plant and seized wood (including fence pickets). Company guards, as well as the Coal and Iron police and armed workers were waiting for trouble. When two older picketers tried to pull boards off the fence, a young man helped. He was shot and died where he stood. Thousands of shots were fired by the plant's defenders, even as the crowd ran. Three men were killed and a number were wounded. One of the dead was a man who had no association with the strike. He was an Edgar Thompson employee whose

wife had begged him to stay home that day. Although he had not gone into work, he grew restless and went to investigate what was going on at the plant. The Industrial Board of the Department of Labor and Industry dispatched investigators who concluded that the men's deaths were not accidents. Those who had fired on the crowd had shot to kill rather than to warn the picketers. No arrests were made, and they were thought to have acted out of excitement rather than malice.

After the deaths at the Edgar Thompson plant, the government sent in troops to restore order to the area. Striker leaders, rioters and radicals were arrested en masse. The strike was more or less at an end by May 9, when the president of Westinghouse told the striking workers that unless all employees were at work the next morning they would lose the benefits that they had accrued under the compensation and pension system.

The press, by and large, blamed the strike on foreign-born men and women. The implication was that native-born Americans were happy with the status quo and were more invested in the current system than immigrants. They would never resort to strikes and violence to achieve their ends. However untrue this may have been, immigrants were an easy scapegoat.

A second notable strike occurred on September 17, 1917, when 300 workers did not show up for work at Jones and Laughlin's Eliza Furnace, prompting the closure of four furnaces and stopping nearly 1,000 other workers from doing their jobs. The initial 300 to 400 strikers were convinced to strike by 130 other workers who were temporarily laid off because Jones and Laughlin abandoned the construction project they were working on. A few days later, the striking employees voted to "call out the workmen in all departments and plants and make the strike general." By then, an assistant foreman had joined the strike, and 5,000 were out of work. The strikers soon formed a list of demands: increased wages (twenty-five cents an hour), guaranteed eight-hour workdays and time-and-a-half pay for holidays and overtime.

By September 23, the striking workers had gained the help of the American Federation of Labor (AFL) and Andrew McNamara, a national organizer. In a statement, McNamara said the strike was a "bona fide trade movement of the American Federation of Labor," which frightened other steel companies. According to the *New York Times*, the steel industry in Pittsburgh had been an "open shop for more than a generation, despite many attempts to organize it." The steel manufacturers, as well as the American government, had been hoping for a lack of disturbances during the war. Attempts to unionize Jones and Laughlin also went against what companies had been promised. One steel company official told the *New York Times* that the administration had received promises from the AFL that no one would attempt to unionize nonunion workers until after the war. The AFL's involvement in Jones and Laughlin's strike might also be the reason that United States Steel chose to raise its employees' wages in late September. Many, including Francis Feehan of the Department of Labor, believed that the strikers were unpatriotic or even committing acts of treason because of the plant's war contracts. However, President Wilson, Secretary Baker and Samuel Gompers of the AFL all sent telegrams that pledged the loyalty of the striking men. The strikers contended that since Jones and Laughlin had withdrawn from the Council on National Defense because of the passage of the Food Bill, it was not disloyal to strike.

Jones and Laughlin promised every striking man his job back as well as a 10 percent pay increase for every employee. Slowly, the men began to return back to work. Forty returned on September 26. The next day men had stopped picketing, and so many returned that Jones and Laughlin could have reopened some of the idle departments. They chose to wait, however, until they were sure the strikers would not cause any disturbances. By the end of the month, it appears that all the rest of the strikers had gone back to work.

The American government also chose to reward industrial workers. Starting September 1, 1918, each worker engaged in war work would be eligible to get a special badge for his or her service. The *Pittsburg Press* explains that "this move to extend official recognition to civil war workers is responsive to the general acknowledgement that those who are steadily producing war supplies are taking a vital part in the prosecution of the war, second only to the part played by the men in actual contact with the enemy." Four consecutive months of war production earned a worker a bronze badge, which could be earned by using time worked before September 1. The other badge, which was to be cast from the same die as the bronze one in a different metal (probably silver), was earned for eight months of work. The second badge could only be earned for work after September 1, although it is unclear whether anyone earned these badges as the war ended in November. The *Pittsburg Press* points out that thousands of Pittsburgh workers would be eligible for at least one of those badges.

Who were the war workers? Immigrants, as discussed earlier in this chapter, made up a large number of workers. They had always made up a large part of the labor force. However, between men leaving to serve in the war and the stoppage of immigration, companies needed to expand their pools of workers. Some of the new workers were working-class women who left their jobs as servants for the higher paying factory jobs. Policemen and firefighters also left their posts for the factories for the same reason. Others were African American migrants from the South. The promise of higher paying industrial work caused Pittsburgh's black population to rise from twenty-five to fifty-five thousand people. Elsewhere in Allegheny County, places such as Carnegie, Aliquippa, Rankin, Braddock, McKeesport and Clarion saw their African American population rise from five thousand to over twenty thousand.

This pattern of migration is typical of what occurred in most northern industrial centers. The World War I period is the first wave of what became known as the Great Migration. Between about 1915 and until about 1970, over six million African Americans left the South in search of new opportunities in the North and Midwest. During the Great War, with European immigration practically at a standstill, African Americans were able fill new factory positions that would have normally been filled by immigrants. Economic hardships in the South as well as Jim Crow laws caused them to seek better opportunities in the North.

Word of mouth as well as advertisements in African American newspapers stressed the economic opportunities in the North. Companies also sent African American and white employment agents south to recruit potential migrants for work in the industries. Industries had deals worked out with the railroads in which the migrant workers would receive "free" transportation north. Upon reaching Pittsburgh, the workers would allow the companies to take money out of their paycheck in order to pay for their travel.

Southern whites were not happy with losing cheap African American labor. They would sometimes resort to threats and intimidations in order to maintain the status quo. In 1917, for example, a Pennsylvania Railroad employment agent attempted to bring two hundred African Americans from Shreveport, Louisiana, to Pittsburgh. The local police chief and a sheriff met the agent and warned him that it was illegal to recruit laborers away from Louisiana and that failure to abandon his plans would result in his arrest. That was enough to get him to go home without the migrant workers.

Most of the work that African American migrants found upon reaching Pittsburgh was unskilled work requiring only physical strength. It was exceptionally hard, hot and dangerous work with long days for everyone who worked in the mills and the plants, but the new migrants often received the worst jobs. They worked in labor gangs in the open hearth and manned the blast furnaces. At AM Byers Company, they were assigned to the galvanizing department, where zinc was used to coat wrought-iron pipes, exposing them to acid fumes that could affect their health.

They also faced hostility and discrimination from their white co-workers as well as their bosses. White workers often refused to work with their African American counterparts. White foremen were harder on them as well. For example, at Jones and Laughlin's By-Products plant, a white foreman from the South would fire African American workers for no reason and replace them with foreign-born ones. In order to combat this problem, managers did hire some African American foremen to head departments that were predominantly black. However, these foremen could not shield the members of their crews from discrimination because they were subject to white bosses.

In many cases the move north did improve African Americans' economic statuses. A University of Pittsburgh survey conducted in 1918 found that of the 453 migrants surveyed, before coming to Pittsburgh 56 percent of them had earned wages below two dollars a day. In Pittsburgh, only 5 percent of those men had such low wages. At the same time, 62 percent earned between two and three dollars a day, something that only 25 percent had done in the South. But these new migrants also had to face inadequate housing.

Pittsburgh was already facing a housing problem, and its steel companies did not plan on the large number of migrants who would come north. Both in the city and the surrounding towns, living space was limited. Companies purchased housing facilities to rent to their new workers, and in some cases, they hastily constructed houses for them. Other companies converted railroad cars into sleeping spaces by equipping them with bunks and trashcans. In other cases, buildings that had previously been condemned were reopened. Men and women in boardinghouses would often use the same bed and work different shifts. By 1918, 50,000 men and women, both white and black and among the city's poorest residents, lived in the deplorable conditions in boardinghouses. Overcrowding made African American migrants and other poor workers more susceptible to diseases such as pneumonia, many laying untreated in their bunkhouses and dying unnoticed. For example, between January and July 1915, only 64 African Americans died of respiratory ailments; 183 died from January to July 1917, a 200 percent increase. African Americans, particularly new migrants, were too poor to get treatment in many cases. This led to a startling statistic: 50 percent more African Americans died in Pittsburgh in 1917 than were born.

The new African American migrants also found a city that was rife with racial discrimination. Certain public facilities would not serve blacks. For example, the only downtown restaurant that was open to them was the basement concessionaire in Rosenbaum's Department store. Added to that, there was a divide within the African American community as a whole. "Old Pittsburgh," lighter skinned African Americans who often had better jobs (servants, for instance) and who had obtained (or whose children had obtained) a college education were often inhospitable to the new, poorer, southern migrants. While many stayed, many of the African American migrants found that life in Pittsburgh was not what they had thought it was going to be. Some went back to the South while others found new opportunities in other northern cities.

CHAPTER THREE

TENSION AND DISSENT IN THE STEEL CITY

S hortly after Congress declared war, the superintendent of Pittsburgh public schools complained to the *Pittsburg Press*, "It isn't a question of cost, although prices [for American flags] have jumped three hundred to four hundred percent. We cannot obtain an American flag at any cost; they are simply unobtainable [*sic*]." Before the United States entered the war, a five- by eight-foot flag would have cost $1.50. Shortly before the article was written, the superintendent had been offered a small number of them. They were $14.00 each. Pittsburgh was not only brimming with patriotism but with capitalism at its finest.

However, despite the (often literal) flag waving, there were tensions boiling beneath the surface due in part to Pittsburgh's large German immigrant population. Take for example the story of Theodore Cossman. Cossman was a fifty-year-old owner of the Wonderland movie theater on Penn Avenue. On April 13, 1917, he decided to exercise his constitutional right to free speech and made an antiwar speech, inciting the crowd of several hundred against him. Riot police were called to disperse the crowd and to arrest Cossman. He was charged with a high misdemeanor and held on a $10,000 bond. Word travelled quickly enough, and while he was being held in an alderman's office, another mob formed outside. They demanded Cossman and threw bricks. This second riot was eventually broken up.

A few days after Cossman's arrest, John Hirmunk, a proud Austrian citizen, was out near his home in Homestead. According to the *Pittsburg Press*, Hirmunk wore a picture of the Kaiser on his jacket and loudly

The British tank Britannia arriving in Pittsburgh on April 27, 1918. It is estimated that the tank was seen by one million Americans when it was displayed on Flagstaff Hill in Schenley Park the next day. The tank was used as a propaganda piece to drum up enlistment. *Courtesy of the Heinz History Center.*

proclaimed his love for his homeland. However, on April 16, he ran into another Homestead man, John Malsok, who proudly wore his American flag. Hirmunk reportedly made a remark about how he would be fighting for Germany. This was enough provocation for Malsok to dish out what the article calls a severe beating. Both men were arrested on charges of disorderly conduct. Burgess Joseph S. Stewart gave Hirmunk a choice: pay a ten-dollar fine and court costs or go to the workhouse. Malsok was not punished at all. Stewart instead praised him for dealing with Hirmunk so efficiently, saying, "Persons insulting the American flag should have all the stuffings beaten out of them—you did right."

By May 1917, tensions were running extremely high in the Pittsburgh area. Pennsylvania's National Guard had been called in to protect local plants, railroads and factories from German sabotage. May 17 seemed like just any other day for the young guardsmen stationed in Port Perry (near Braddock, Pennsylvania) when they had lunch at a local restaurant owned by Carl Miller. The restaurant was a favorite among the guardsmen, and most of the fifty-one men who ate there were young, in their late teens and early twenties, and healthy. However, around two o'clock that afternoon Lieutenant William F. Corcoran fell ill after eating at Miller's restaurant. He made it to the Pullman car that the soldiers were using as a headquarters and said, "Well boys, I'm very sick—I believe I'm done for." He waved to his men and said, "I've got my last call" before slumping to the ground. Although his panicked men called the doctors, he was dead before they arrived. Forty-nine of the other men who ate at Miller's restaurant also became ill and were rushed to West Penn and Braddock Hospitals as doctors tried to determine what had caused the sickness.

Papers nationwide were buzzing with the news, and cries of poisoning were running rampant. The *Philadelphia Inquirer*'s headline the day after Corcoran's death confirmed everyone's worst fears, reading, "German Plot Hint Follows Poisoning of Soldier's Food". The paper reported that, "It was freely predicted that a sensation will likely spring out of the case, inasmuch as it is reported that prominent Germans are at the bottom of it."

While breaking the story, the *Pittsburg Press* even went so far as to report local rumors that a week before the men fell ill, one of them was playing the piano in the restaurant when a woman requested a German song. When he told her that it was inappropriate, given the current climate, she was indignant. The next day the *Inquirer* reported that it was Corcoran at the piano and that the mysterious woman was a member of the Miller family. Carl Miller was arrested and placed in military custody almost immediately following Corcoran's death, and his restaurant placed under military guard. No one was allowed in or out until the mystery was thoroughly investigated.

On May 18, the *Pittsburg Press* reported that the state chemist Professor F.T. Aschman believed the cause of Corcoran's death and the others' illnesses was impure milk, which Miller had used to make pudding. State officials had warned Miller that his milk was impure on April 12, but he kept using it to disastrous consequences. Although the milk was likely the culprit, it does not appear to have been widely accepted. By May 19, Fire Marshal Thomas Pfarr became involved in the investigation. Apparently Corcoran had been investigating some fires at Miller's restaurant before he was killed. According to Pfarr, Corcoran was also considering closing the restaurant down because Miller served liquor and hired pretty waitresses in order to attract the troops to his establishment. By May 20, Pfarr was telling the *Pittsburg Press* that he was sure the fires and Corcoran's death were connected.

By the end of June, the *Philadelphia Inquirer* was reporting another sensational twist in the case. Corcoran, days before his death, had punished a number of his men for breaking the rules by forcing them to eat only bread and water.

The *Inquirer* reports that the investigation was going to center on them and speculated that they might have killed him. By early July, the coroner's jury report was released. The jury had finished analyzing Corcoran's stomach contents and determined that he died of an unknown poison. It speculated that the cause was ptomaine poisoning (food poisoning).

The last reference to the story comes on July 9, in Philadelphia's *Evening Public Ledger*. The bulk of the article discusses another guardsmen from Corcoran's company, who made the unfortunate decision to stand up on a roller coaster at Kennywood, hit his head and died at Braddock Hospital. The last lines of the article discuss Corcoran's death briefly, calling it mysterious. It is very likely that Aschman was correct in his initial suspicions. Corcoran died and his men fell ill because of bad milk. There is no evidence that Miller was anything but a cheap business owner and a poor cook. With the sensational aspects stripped away from the story, the newspapers moved on.

It is clear that Corcoran's death and the intense atmosphere that surrounded it led to the death of another man. In the immediate aftermath, the guards assigned to protect the plants and factories in and around Pittsburgh, for fear of German sabotage, were given strict orders. If anyone tried to enter their area and could not provide the password, they were to try and get them to turn back. If they refused to turn back, they were to be shot dead. Pittsburgher Frank Barnsei attempted to enter a mill yard on the Northside. When he continued into the yard after the soldiers told him to turn back he was shot three times in the head. Although he was still alive on arrival at West Penn Hospital, he was not expected to recover.

This story is symptomatic of the extreme fear that was present in Pittsburgh. Because of its industrial output, many in Pittsburgh feared a German attack. This was only exasperated by the amount of German American Pittsburghers. This fear led to an intolerance of anyone and anything that was perceived to be anything less than 100 percent American.

A year later, in May 1918, a man lost his life because of a fight over the flag. Fifty-eight-year-old Adolph Steding was a member of Pittsburgh's large German community. He owned a store on Smithfield Street where he dealt in German books, fancy stationery, dolls and albums. During a visit to the Schenley Hotel in 1918, he made some comments which William Dilworth construed as pro-German. Dilworth, a member of a prominent Pittsburgh grocery and iron family, took issue with Steding, calling him pro-German. In 1918, those were fighting words. Steding defended himself using vile language and the argument escalated until, according to the *Pittsburg Press*, Dilworth told him, "I'll knock your block off!" Steding insisted that the

THE ARSENAL OF THE ALLIES

two men resolve their differences with their fists, calling Dilworth a coward when he backed off. Finally, Dilworth told him to meet him at the Bigelow monument in Schenley Park the next morning and tried to leave the bar. Steding followed him out, however, and according to Dilworth, tried to punch him. Dilworth hit Steding in the jaw, knocking him to the ground. He said that the fight ended there. However, Steding told his daughter Elsa that Dilworth jumped on him, breaking his leg. Steding's leg was fractured, which led to its amputation. The amputation led to a hemorrhage, which resulted in the man's death four months later in August 1918.

There is no indication that Steding's death was the result of anything more than a drunken brawl. Whether or not Dilworth broke Steding's leg, he certainly did not intend for him to die. He was as shocked as anyone else by the outcome. Regardless, the role he played in Steding's death was something that he needed to live with for the rest of his life. This and other such fights were not isolated incidents but rather examples of the dark undertone to Pittsburgh's superpatriotism. To be sympathetic to the German cause meant aligning yourself with America's barbarous enemies. Any sign of disunity, any sign of anything other than intense American patriotism, had no place in the city. Immigrant or not, you were expected to conform and at least give lip service to American ideals. If you did not, plenty of Pittsburghers thought that you deserved what you got.

These sentiments were supported by the American government, which would occasionally make arrests based on allegations of anti-American speech. In late September 1918, wealthy German immigrant (and naturalized American citizen) Charles F. Banning and University of Pittsburgh German professor George F. Stoecklein were arrested on suspicion of sedition. Members of the German club, which the men belonged to, were also rounded up and interrogated in order to help the government's case against Banning. What Banning was alleged to have done was to have made negative comments about the United States and its government and to have expressed a desire that Germany would win the war. He had apparently been under surveillance by the Justice Department since making a trip to Germany in 1914 (the same year he became a naturalized American citizen). Banning was arrested as an enemy alien and imprisoned in Georgia. He was imprisoned for the duration of the war but was released in January 1919.

Pittsburghers did not limit themselves to fighting perceived enemies within the city. Patriotic Pittsburgh organizations also blocked from entering the city those whose sympathies they felt lay with Germany. The most notable case was that of the famous violinist Fritz Kreisler. Kreisler was from Austria.

In 1914, at the outbreak of the war, he served for a mere six weeks in the Austrian army on the Russian front. He was not a volunteer for the army; he was drafted. After receiving a wound, he was released from the army. It is important to remember that when he served, the United States had not yet entered the war. After being released from service, he came to America, where he had previously toured. He sent some of the money he earned back to Austria to help support his seventy-four-year-old father, who had suffered a stroke. He also sent some of his earnings to Russian and Serbian orphans whose fathers his wife had nursed when she was on the front lines of the war. By his own admission, the majority of his earnings went to the Brotherhood of Artists, which supported artists who could not make a living regardless of nationality. However, as soon as the United States entered the war, he made sure that he funneled no money to anyone who lived in a country that was now America's enemy.

This did not stop Pittsburghers from blocking his concert. Several organizations in the city, including the Daughters of the American Revolution, took issue with his foreign ties when he was scheduled to play in the city in November 1917. They believed that it would be unpatriotic to allow a man who had served in the Austrian army to perform as public entertainment. Pressure on city officials to cancel the concert, which was to take place in Carnegie Music Hall, mounted. The day before the concert, the director of public safety ordered the Pittsburgh Police Department to deny him a concert permit. His manager was given a choice: cancel the concert or be barred from playing. They cancelled the engagement. Pittsburgh was one of the first cities to stop him from performing, but it was not the last. By the end of November 1917, Kreisler quit touring for the duration of the war, not returning to the stage until October 1919. His career did recover, and eventually, his ties to Austria ceased to matter. He performed at many concerts for war charities during the Second World War and became an American citizen.

Intense nativism, as well as anti-German sentiments, led to the birth of the American Protective League (also known as the APL or simply the League), which became one of the most controversial civilian organizations during the war. Although it was founded and based out of Chicago, there was an active branch in Pittsburgh. Members of the group were extreme nativists who viewed every German as a potential agent of the Kaiser. In Emerson Hough's 1919 authorized history of the APL, *The Web*, he describes the threat that plagued America: "German-Americans never cared for America at all…they were never anything but German. They used America, they

This cartoon, published in the *Cartoon Book* in 1918 by the U.S. Treasury Department to promote the Third Liberty Loan Campaign, captures anti-German sentiments in the United States. *Courtesy of the Heinz History Center.*

never loved her. They clung to their old language, their old customs and cared not for ours. They prospered because they would live as we would not live. It would be wrong to call them all bad and a folly to call them all good. As a class they were clannish…Open and covert action was taken on both sides of the Atlantic to bring America into line." This statement, while a very good summary of the nativist position, only has a kernel of truth to it. I will discuss German Americans in greater depth later in this book. However, most German Americans of course were not agents of the German government hoping to overthrow the American one. Some of the German Americans the APL discussed were not even immigrants, but second- and third-generation Americans of German descent who had grown up in tightknit German communities. Yes, German Americans did cling to their culture. There were German newspapers in all major cities with a large German population (Pittsburgh included); there were German neighborhoods with German churches, businesses and cultural organizations. German children learned to be bilingual. But the same can be said of every major immigrant group. Germans were also one of this country's oldest immigrant groups, and many were respected members of their communities as well as members of a powerful political lobby. All of this, however, bred fear.

The APL saw itself as "a silent, unknown army of more than a quarter million of the most loyal and intelligent citizens of America, who did indeed spring to arms over night. It fought battles, saved lives, saved cities, saved treasures, defended the flag, apprehended countless traitors, did its own tremendous share in winning the war. It saved America. It did protect. It was the league." Right or wrong, it was a powerful organization in America that often worked with the federal government to keep tabs on Germans and other undesirables. The Pittsburgh branch's office, for example, shared a building with the BI as well as other government agencies. While it was only supposed to assist in routine investigations so that agents were free to do more important tasks, its members (all volunteers) often saw this as an official government sanction. Vigilantism was not uncommon. Neither was trampling on civil liberties and the Bill of Rights.

The APL and its members might have done reprehensible things, but that does not mean that they were evil men. In 1917, many would have told you just the opposite. They were heavily screened and came primarily from Pittsburgh middle and upper classes. League leaders were among Pittsburgh's most prominent citizens. While this does not excuse any abuse of power, they were products of their time and their class. Many undoubtedly believed in their mission. They believed that immigrants, (especially Germans during the war) were suspect of subversion. They were inherently suspicious of anyone and anything that did not fit into their view of Americanism. More than anything, they felt that it was their duty for God and country to protect America from German subversion.

The Pittsburgh APL division was begun by a Pittsburgh businessman named John W. Weibley. It covered twenty-seven counties in western

Pennsylvania, and within a short time of its founding, the APL had active agents in every town and city within its division. In Pittsburgh, there were agents in every precinct and in ethnic neighborhoods, on every block. While the members themselves were unpaid, their activities were funded by Pittsburgh industries. At the outbreak of the war, while the government was stationing troops to protect Pittsburgh's plants, the APL investigated over twenty-five thousand cases of suspected German spies already at work in them. All the men and women the APL investigated were innocent.

Although the APL's original mission was targeted at Germans, its activities soon spread beyond German Americans. For example, it was illegal to sell liquor to soldiers while they were in uniform or within certain areas near army camps in the city. League members, for whatever reason, decided that an African American man selling iced tea near one of the camps must be breaking the liquor laws. An operative approached the man to buy a quart of tea. As soon as the purchase was made, the operative arrested the vendor. The tea was tested and found to be just that—iced tea. While Pittsburgh's APL chief Weibley described this as a humorous story, one can only assume the poor man they arrested would disagree.

The Radical Left also found itself under attack. Socialist and others deemed "anarchist" or "radicals" were often subject to League scrutiny because they opposed the war and the draft. The League credited itself for breaking up a ring and arresting its radical leader right before he was to address a meeting. Hough says, "The facts that the plans of the scheme were so well known to the League cooled the ardor of the malcontents."

In fact, those who were attempting to evade the draft (and those who helped them) soon became among the League's primary targets. Two lawyers advertising legal advice on how to evade the draft were given a warning while two Italian men who were planning on filling out questionnaires for men so they could evade the draft were arrested. One of the cases, which the Pittsburgh APL was the most proud of, was the capture of University of Pittsburgh student Walter L. Hirschberg.

Hirschberg was a conscientious objector, who allegedly sent the draft board a declaration of rights when he registered and "maintained an attitude of defiance towards the government." He was investigated as a potential problem, but he soon left Pittsburgh for New York City. There, he was located and locked in a hotel until evidence could be found against him. He soon escaped and fled to Chicago, where he was discovered by a Pittsburgh APL member, who returned him to Pittsburgh at gunpoint. Hirschberg was later court-martialed and sentenced to twenty years in jail.

The APL also took part in the March 1918 slacker raids in Pittsburgh. "Slacker" was the term used to describe draft dodgers, and they were becoming a nationwide problem. In January 1918, an estimated 50,000 men had deserted the army, and 300,000 men were draft delinquents. Something clearly had to be done. The BI and the War Department were both interested in trying to solve the problem. The BI was to use APL members to carry out raids to capture the slackers. Meanwhile, Pittsburgh Public Safety director Charles B. Prichard ordered that the slackers in Pittsburgh be rounded up early in March, believing there to be hundreds in the city. He claimed that Pittsburgh's slackers were men posing as traveling salesmen as well as the sons of the wealthy.

On March 2, 1918 (which was a Saturday night), squads of Pittsburgh police, federal agents and "special police" swarmed around men on street corners, in hotels, boardinghouses, cafes, pool rooms and clubs. Those men out for a night on the town without their registration cards were carted off to jail amid the jeers of the crowd. Those that could have friends or family bring their registration cards to jail were released. The raids were continued over the next few nights, and soon, most of the city jails were filling up. For example, out of 901 prisoners in the Allegheny County jail, 503 of them had been arrested in the raids. As men continued to be arrested, an old armory was converted into a guardhouse to hold them, guarded by federal troops from New York City.

Many of the men arrested were innocent. Some had registered for the draft and just had not received their cards yet. Others were too young or too old. Some were not even American, so therefore, not eligible. During the raids, two men were arrested for impersonating federal officials even though they were wearing civilian clothes. Abuse and humiliation of suspected slackers (particularly by "special police") was not uncommon. Although federal courts would later condemn the warrantless mass arrests, the Pittsburgh slacker raids set a wartime precedent. They were repeated in other cities such as New York later that year.

Patriotism was not the only thing that caused strain within the city during the war. Many of Pittsburgh's firefighters and police enlisted in the armed services as soon as America entered the war. Others left their jobs for the high wages offered by industries, leaving a labor shortage in Pittsburgh's police and fire departments. This meant longer hours for those who remained, while still making the same amount they did before the war. Meanwhile, living costs were at an all-time high. Left with little choice, in 1918, the police and firefighters petitioned the city for a pay increase. The city increased the wages of the police by fifteen dollars a month but ignored the firefighters' request.

After the firefighters threatened to strike, the city agreed to raise their pay by five dollars a month. Incised by what they saw as a slap in the face, the firefighters voted by an overwhelming majority to strike. It is important to remember what a firefighters' strike meant for the city. Pittsburgh was called "the Arsenal of the World" because it was a center of wartime activity. Several plants were manufacturing explosives. An out-of-control fire in the wrong area could mean massive explosion and dead civilians. Added to that, there was the constant fear that the German spies would attempt to sabotage Pittsburgh's plants and mills. Tensions were extremely high when, at noon on August 24, 1918, the firefighters went on strike, taking all but one fire alarm operator with them. A fire alarm operator on the North Side, Elmer Loomis, refused to leave with his co-workers. He promised to eat and sleep next to his alarm until the strike was resolved.

Mayor Edward V. Babcock realized he had a problem on his hands. He called for volunteers and three hundred student soldiers from the University of Pittsburgh and Carnegie Tech left their Schenley Park training camp to protect the factories and man the firehouses. The alarm systems were placed into the hands of repairmen who were not a part of the strike. Police were called in to guard engine houses. The city also took the steps to notify draft boards of the names of the firefighters, many of whom had claimed draft exemptions because of their occupation. However, the situation threatened to turn extremely serious. Crowds of Pittsburghers sympathetic to the firefighters' plight gathered at engine houses bringing with them the threat of riots.

Meanwhile, three fires broke out in Pittsburgh. Two were not serious and were extinguished by a variety of volunteers, many of them factory workers. However, a fire on Penn Avenue was much larger. Although they might have wanted more money, the striking firefighters were not about to let half the city burn down to prove a point. So they rushed to the scene of the fire, only to learn that the volunteers had managed to control the blaze.

The strike itself lasted a total of six hours. When word of the strike reached Washington, D.C., the army and navy realized what a disruption in Pittsburgh could mean for the war effort. President Wilson ordered the War Labor Board, a commission created to settle strikes in war industries, to intervene. They sent a telegram, promising that if the firefighters returned to work, representatives of the board would intervene on their behalf. While it is unclear whether or not the firefighters received a pay raise, the promise from Washington seemed to satisfy them. There does not seem to have been any other threats to strike.

CHAPTER FOUR

IMMIGRANT COMMUNITIES

Pittsburgh, like many industrial centers in the United States, was a city of immigrants by the time the archduke and his wife were gunned down in Sarajevo. As discussed earlier, immigrants flocked to the city in large numbers because of the economic opportunities offered by the Pittsburgh area's mills, factories and mines. Generally, these newcomers settled in ethnic enclaves where they formed ethnic societies in which they could speak their own languages and preserve as much of their old cultures as possible. While this often led to heightened tensions, it also gave the city a unique ethnic flavor and a level of importance in many immigrant communities. This was especially true of Pittsburgh's Polish American population.

As a result, in 1912, Pittsburgh became the headquarters of the very influential Polish Falcons of America. Pittsburgher Dr. Teofil A. Starzynski became its president. Although Poland as a country had not been on the map since 1795—it had been divided between Russia, Prussia (later a part of a unified Germany) and Austria (later part of the Austro-Hungarian empire)—nationalism among the Polish people did not die. Many Polish Americans, including Starzynski, dreamt of seeing an independent Poland.

In order to achieve Polish independence, many Polish leaders felt that military action was needed. So as early as 1907, Starzynski advocated for forming rifle clubs among Polish Falcon members. He also wanted to form military and gymnastic schools in order to train the next generation of Polish military leaders. As tensions rose between the United States and Germany, Polish Americans saw an unprecedented opportunity. On February 10,

1915, the movement gained support when a Polish Falcon delegation led by Starzynski visited the White House. President Wilson became the first world leader to support Polish independence, saying, "When the United States shall sit at the peace conference all efforts shall be made to see that Poland is independent again."

Emboldened by Wilson's statements, Starzynski encouraged military training groups to be established on a permanent basis in January the following year. He also called for the Falcons to sponsor rifle clubs and first-aid courses. By the fall, meetings in Pittsburgh produced a training school for officers with a $10,000 budget. In November and December 1916, Physical Instructors from all over the country met in Pittsburgh for "leadership training." In reality, they were given basic training on military tactics, which they then spread to members in their local areas. Because the United States was still neutral, these courses were called physical instruction rather than military instruction.

By April 1, 1917, when America's entrance into Europe's war seemed inevitable, a convention was held in the Southside to decide what steps to take when war was declared. Following Pittsburgh mayor Armstrong's speech, the delegates debated the feasibility of a Polish army. Noted Polish patriot, composer and pianist Ignacy Jan Paderewski arrived in Pittsburgh on April 2 to great fanfare. People filled the Falcon's hall to hear his opinion on the matter. He encouraged loyalty to the United States, saying, "I have full confidence in the United States, in its future and in their ideals upon which this great nation was built. Particularly let us be loyal to President Woodrow Wilson, the champion of the downtrodden nations." But he pointed out that the future of Poland rested with those Polish Americans willing to fight for it. He said, "To form a [Polish] army under the stars and stripes, to fight alongside the Allies against Imperial Germany which has infringed on the rights of almost all nations of the world...permit me to spend a wire to President Wilson offering an army of 100,000 men." His speech was greeted with applause by the packed house. The convention voted to approve the army's formation and, furthermore, that the army and the training courses it would offer be open to all who wanted to fight for Poland, not just Polish nationals.

The U.S. government, however, was not eager to approve the army for several reasons. America needed all able-bodied young men willing to fight to enlist in its own army. The government feared it could also set a precedent for other nationalistic groups to form their own armies. Furthermore, to openly support the Polish call to arms risked antagonizing Russia, a key member of the Allied forces. Despite this, the Polish Falcons opened the first national recruiting office in Pittsburgh in October 1917 in the hopes that the American government would change its position. Hope was renewed in March 1918 when Bolshevik Russia signed a treaty with the Central powers. This led the way for the creation of Polish legions in Allied armies. France led the way in June, and while some Americans flocked to France to join, many believed an American army would soon follow. Eventually, the American and British government recognized a Polish government operating out of New York. They also allowed for the recruitment of a Polish army in America, which was to be trained in Canadian camps.

The backbone of recruitment efforts was formed by Polish Catholic churches. Recruitment meetings were often religious festivals. Not only did clergy members take an active role in recruitment, but also three Pittsburgh priests even left their flocks to join the effort. When recruitment officially ended February 15, 1919, out of the 38,088 Americans who enlisted in the Polish army, 3,000 were from Pittsburgh. Many of them left well-paying jobs in the factories to do so. After their service was completed and Poland was an independent country again, many of these men wished to return to the United States. In the 1920s, the Polish government paid for the passage of all men who wished to return to America.

Despite this, the one immigrant group most affected by World War I was the German Americans. Although by the dawn of the twentieth century they were among Pittsburgh's most prominent citizens, the Germans assimilated on their own terms. They considered themselves American in every way that mattered while still seeking to preserve the culture and heritage from their fatherland. German Protestant churches conducted services in German, although the Catholic Mass was still primarily in Latin. Churches in German neighborhoods, such as St. Mary's in Allegheny City (now Pittsburgh's Northside), preached homilies in German. German newspapers were established. German clubs and societies were formed, as were German beneficial societies.

Although members of a culturally rich and distinctive community, the German Americans, both in Pittsburgh and nationally, were poised to undergo a change by the beginning of the twentieth century. Decreased immigration from Germany meant that in order to preserve the institutions they built here, German Americans needed to ensure their cultural values were passed down to their children. Exacerbating the issue, nativist groups cried for them to assimilate completely into the greater Anglicized American culture. As a whole, the community also found itself on the wrong side of the debate over the prohibition of alcohol. For many in the community, Prohibition sought to destroy not only their cultural drink of choice but also their very livelihoods. Pittsburgh alone had several breweries founded and owned by German Americans, the most prominent example being Pittsburgh Brewing Company.

The National German-American Alliance (known as the Alliance), founded in Philadelphia in 1901, was a nationwide organization that sought to tackle issues such as Prohibition, preserving and spreading German culture to second- and third-generation German Americans, immigration and the relations between Germany and America. It was a federation of existing organizations, which were grouped together in local alliances. These local alliances made up state branches, which together formed the national alliance. In order to gain membership, one had to pay dues and be a citizen of the United States. This came as much from a love of their new homeland as it did from common sense. Citizens could form a voting bloc, which could, in theory, influence policy. It was this desire, compounded by World War I, which led to the organization's eventual downfall in 1918. Locally, the Alliance's Allegheny County Branch encompassed 143 local German societies and had over twenty thousand members at its height in 1918. To put that in perspective, in 1914, the New York City Branch claimed to have twenty-four thousand members and the entire state of Illinois only twenty thousand.

World War I was a watershed moment within the German American community as a whole, and especially in Pittsburgh. When war broke out in Europe, German Americans stood firmly behind their fatherland. On August 2, 1914, the day after negotiations between Germany and Russia broke down and war was declared, the *Pittsburg Press* spoke with local German Americans. The newspaper concluded that the local community was not surprised. In fact, "the pending clash on the field of battle between the forces of Emperor William [the paper curiously chose to Anglicize Wilhem] and the great hordes of soldiery that will rally about the banner of Czar Nicholas has been foreseen for some time by the intelligent Americanized Germans. Russia's ambition and aggressive measures have been greatly resented and the only surprise has been…that the differences and sufficient causes of war between the two nations did not come to a head sooner. Emperor William is given credit with having displayed remarkable patience." Local German Americans were convinced that Germany would win. They believed that Germany had a superior army. The newspaper goes on to say that the news that Germany has "taken a firm and final stand in defense for its rights and in defense of its honor as a nation and its standing among first class powers was greeted enthusiastically." The paper expected, given the enthusiasm of local Germans that many would go back to fight for the Kaiser. Because as loyal as they were to America, "the love for their old home country is deeply rooted in their hearts." The article concludes with H.C. Bloedel's, president of the Allegheny County Branch of the National German-American Alliance, explanation that "German subjects all over the world will be notified and called upon for aid, through the German consuls."

As the above article demonstrates, Pittsburgh newspapers were not simply vehicles for anti-German propaganda. In fact, at the beginning of the war, articles in Pittsburgh newspapers portrayed Russians as culturally inferior to their German counterparts. They also reported that Russia was on the verge of civil war, and involvement in a greater European war was a move by the desperate Czar Nicholas II to hang onto power by giving his people a common enemy. This was before America's involvement; by the time America entered the war, Pittsburgh's English-language newspapers had changed their portrayal of Germany and Germans. The German forces were often portrayed as Huns involved in a costly war against democracy (represented by England, France and, later, the United States). The change was, of course, gradual. Germany's invasion of neutral Belgium started the downward spiral of negative press. Allied reports of war crimes, such as destroying villages and raping women, only hindered the German cause. Germany also made a number of other missteps, culminating in the sinking of the *Lusitania* and the Zimmerman Telegram, which drove the United States closer to war. The reaction of the German American community to these events shaped the city and the country for years to come.

Although it might not have been accurate, from the beginning of the war, many of the Allegheny County German American community viewed the English-language press as being pro-Allies. German Americans believed it their duty—to both their motherlands—to combat American lies. Local Alliance leader H.C. Bloedel stated in the meeting on August 23, 1914, "In these sad hours of trial, in which Germania is engaged in its most momentous struggle for 'to be or not to be,' fighting for its very existence, in a war wrought upon them by hate, contest, and the lowest instincts, it is no more than natural and proper that Germania's children in foreign countries be not merely onlookers of this titanic struggle, but do their best in noble sacrificing spirit and come to their kinsfolks' aid in their time of vicissitude and trial. It is an elevating spectacle to see the entire

H.C. Bloedel, president of the local chapter of the National German American Alliance. *Courtesy of the Heinz History Center.*

German-American press and people unified in their efforts to oppose the malice of the lying and hateful press and lay open their infamy." Pamphlets the Alliance published told the German side of the struggle. From the beginning, however, it was clear that the Alliance and many German Americans were still maintaining a distance from the greater American society while seeking to influence it.

However, it is important to remember that despite their distress over the German cause, the Alliance also encouraged its members to stay focused on American issues. Bloedel reminded those who attended the Alliance's October meeting that "we must not become blind to the earnest problems to be solved in our country of adoption. It is our chief duty to serve this country first…We must always keep in mind the great struggle before us… The law of self-preservation demands that we redouble our energies towards the attainment of our objectives." Bloedel concluded his speech by urging the German Americans to vote together on German issues in the upcoming elections. It worked. All but two of the candidates backed by the Allegheny County Alliance won. Among the issues that Bloedel was concerned about was defeating prohibition.

Fear of nativist elements combining forces against the German Americans also drove Bloedel's October 31, 1915 speech. He said, "The, in Anglo-American circles, generally unveiled hate for all that is 'German' makes it a duty for every German-American to watch over the rights and privileges guaranteed him by the glorious Constitution of the United States, that none of those rights be reduced. No American of German ancestry must be influenced by the animosity shown him by those backing up the ignorant and spiteful yellow press, neither should it have any bearing on his self-respect and self-confidence. Unalterably he must stand up for those ideals and aims helping to develop the welfare of our country by adoption." Understand, Bloedel was not just talking to newly minted Americans born in the fatherland. In order to form the largest possible voting bloc, the Alliance had to appeal to second- and third-generation German Americans. However, his rhetoric and the rhetoric of many members of the Alliance, show a disconnect with these Americans. America, not Germany, was their homeland. They were born here; it was not their adopted country, though they were raised in German communities. They might have learned to speak and read German. As members of the Alliance, they might have been sympathetic to some German causes (particularly defeating Prohibition), but they were Americans, if attempting to navigate two worlds. It's also important to remember that membership in the Alliance, even attending Alliance meetings, did not mean that everyone agreed with the Alliance's goals.

This disconnect between the Alliance and those German Americans born in the United States eventually became problematic. On July 30, 1916, a motion was made at a meeting to publish what the Alliance called the *Domestic Gazette*. It was to be published in English not German. They believed that the influence of "German intellectuality" was vital to America as a nation, accepting that younger German Americans no longer felt the need to speak their parents' language and live in their parents' world. The Alliance hoped that the paper would interest this generation and allow it to be raised with an appreciation and understanding of culture and what it meant to be German. The Alliance believed that other sources published in English that these young people readily read—whether they were novels or newspapers—contained an inherent disrespect for everything German. This, in turn, caused young people to become disrespectful to their parents (perhaps seeing them as outdated and Old World) as well as their parents' culture and fatherland. The *Domestic Gazette*, therefore, "must be bearing the spirit of truth and enlightenment, so as to inspire the present and coming generation, and to shape their conscious so as to make them see their great mission as Americans of German decent. It is theirs and our part to safeguard German intellect and its effect upon American life, *spelling true patriotism*." The *Domestic Gazette* marks a massive shift in the Alliance's thought process. It was certainly meant to help educate young German Americans in their ancestors' culture. But it was almost surely an attempt to combat what was seen as anti-German, pro-Anglican propaganda with pro-German propaganda.

Despite the stated intentions of the publication, Allegheny County U.S attorney E. Lowry Humes took a much more cynical view of the *Domestic Gazette*. The meeting minutes regarding its publication were included in the evidence against the Alliance that he presented during the 1917 U.S. Senate hearings about its activities. Humes said, "I think that these minutes…would indicate that it was for the preservation of unity for any political purposes rather than the preservation of any German ideals." In his view, the Alliance had become a political organization first and foremost and not a cultural one.

One of the most telling examples of the Alliance's attempts to influence mainstream politics was its attempt to change American policy over its neutrality during the war. The issue of American neutrality became an issue among the German American community and remained one until America entered the war. While America had been more than willing to trade with both sides of the conflict, the British made trade with Germany impossible. By November 1914, England had declared the North Sea a war zone and began planting landmines. America remained silent on the issue and the British had successfully restricted American trade to just the Allies.

America's willingness to trade in war materials with the Allied nations was seen as a breach of its neutrality by the German American community. In January 1915, Allegheny County Alliance president Bloedel and others encouraged every citizen, regardless of nationality, to join the protest. Many did. The *New Republic* reported that there was a growing number of Americans uncomfortable with American companies "capitalizing on carnage." Bills to ban the sale of weapons were proposed in Congress. However, it remained the policy of the Wilson administration that trading with the Allies was not a breach of America's neutrality. Without the president's support, measures restricting trade were doomed to fail. This policy would in turn set many German Americans against Wilson.

In August 1915, the Alliance held what would become its last convention. It was held in San Francisco and coincided with the San Francisco Exposition. On the third day, Bloedel, always a firebrand, presented a strongly worded letter to be sent to Wilson. Bloedel denounced Wilson, his policies and where they led the United States: "In the eyes of our contemporaries…and before the tribunal of history we [the United States] stand convicted." Many of his fellow delegates (over six hundred from forty-five states) believed Bloedel's letter went too far. After a fierce debate, several delegates (including six officers) threatened to leave if the letter was adopted and sent. The national president, Charles Hexamer, offered a compromise. An amended letter was sent that simply called on the government to stop supplying weapons to the Allied nations and help bring the war to an end. America, according to the letter, should be a moral light. While Wilson did not respond to this attack, many Americans were growing wary of the Alliance. Attacking the president branded them as pro-German, not pro-neutrality. Added to that, American attitudes were beginning to shift due to other events, such as the sinking of the *Lusitania*.

As America edged closer and closer to war with Germany, the Alliance's showdown with Wilson cumulated in the election of 1916. It was determined to defeat Wilson at all cost. In addition to not liking Wilson or his policies, its greatest fear was that America's financial ties to the Allied nations would cause it to get involved in the war on what it considered to be the wrong side. The Allegheny County Branch took up the call against Wilson admirably. After Bloedel's death in 1916, the new president of the Allegheny County Alliance wasted no time in issuing a telegram to Washington, again protesting the sale of weapons to the Allies. It read in part, "Over 20,000 American citizens, members of the Allegheny County Branch…put forth to protest in the name of true humanity (not sham humanity), against efforts to draw the United States into war. We may, for the protection of our own country, be in dire need of submarines ourselves, and should therefore not destroy our best weapon, merely to help and assist England, our country's worst enemy. No one man seeking eagerly reelection should be permitted to sacrifice American blood and property just to satisfy political whim and aspirations." This telegram showed how out of touch the Alliance was with the majority of Americans. It further served to brand the organization as pro-German, which would prove to be problematic. Being seen as pro-German would undoubtedly taint whichever candidate it backed. It was a gamble and a test of the power of its voting bloc, one that would prove fatal for both its presidential candidate and the Alliance itself.

To make matters worse, the Alliance couldn't even agree on which candidate it wanted to back in 1916. It only knew that it did not want, Wilson or Theodore Roosevelt, who was attempting to make a political comeback. Roosevelt was seen as more pro-English and prowar than Wilson. Because there was no real consensus, the Allegheny County Branch told its members to write in Henry Ford as their presidential nominee. It also presented candidates for Congress who it believed supported German American interests. Eventually, the Allegheny County Branch decided to vote with the rest of the Alliance and support Charles

Hughes, the Republican nominee for president, instead of Ford. Wilson ran on the slogan "He kept us out of the war" and won reelection, in part by capitalizing on Hughes's ties to an organization that was increasingly being seen as an organ of the German government.

Despite the Alliance's losses in the presidential election, the Allegheny County Alliance continued to petition the government for neutrality into 1917. In January, it drew up resolutions that were sent to member of the U.S. Congress as well as Pennsylvania's General Assembly. These resolutions called for an embargo on food exports, in particular, grain to the Allies. By February, however, the *Pittsburg Press* reported that while the Alliance might still be hoping for America's continued neutrality, Louis Ullrich, the local Alliance's president, assured the paper that the Alliance stood firmly behind America in the event of war.

Perhaps the most relevant mouthpiece of the Alliance was Pittsburgh's German newspapers, which included *Volksblatt und Freiheits Freund*. The paper was riddled with pro-German articles concerning the war. It, like the Alliance, took what most Americans considered to be the wrong side on a number of issues. For example, scholar Cheryl Lynn Miller characterizes the newspaper's reaction to the sinking of the *Lusitania* in 1915 as being more impressed with German naval advances than concerned for the loss of American lives. The newspaper pointed out that British actions made German submarine warfare necessary, and the passengers themselves bore some responsibility for their deaths. The paper points out that the passengers should have known that traveling on a British ocean liner was a risk.

Although harsh, *Volksblatt und Freiheits Freund* had a point. Before the ship even left New York City, the German embassy in Washington published a very clear warning, carried in many American newspapers, reminding American travelers that Great Britain and Germany were at war. The warning stated the war zone included the waters surrounding the British Isles and that any ship bearing the flag of one of the Allied countries was at risk of being sunk. Travelers on British ships would do so at their own risk.

In the days following the sinking, *Volksblatt und Freiheits Freund* carried comments made by Colonel Dr. Derberg, an ex-German secretary of state and a propaganda minister sent by the German government to New York City, in which he explains why Germany was within its rights to sink the *Lusitania*. In the article, he alleges that it was not listed as a supply ship and was carrying contraband. Incidentally, this claim was true. The luxury liner was carrying American-made weapons as well as sixty-seven Canadian soldiers. Even so, the majority of the American population was at the loss of

American lives. Reports from the survivors were filling American newspapers all around the country, further horrifying Americans. The sinking of the *Lusitania* was later used as one of the primary reasons for America to enter the war against Germany. Even though more and more Americans were calling for the United States to enter the war after the *Lusitania*, in 1915, that was not a forgone conclusion.

In fact, *Volksblatt und Freiheits Freund* tried it's best to alleviate readers' fears that America would enter the war. It did this in several ways. The newspaper reported that an Idaho senator who was sure that while Americans would mourn their countrymen, they would understand that it was not an attack against the United States. When the paper reported that the German ambassador to the United States expressed his personal sadness at the loss of American life, it also discussed Wilson's potential responses to the tragedy. The paper concluded that for America to cut ties with Germany would be a grave mistake. It asserted that it would have "serious effects on the humanitarian standard that the United States has set forth" and that it might threaten the position of American diplomats in Belgium and endanger relief organizations.

Wilson considered Germany to be responsible for the inexcusable attacks on vessels carrying citizens from a neutral county and that the German government's warnings, no matter how well publicized, did not justify the act of sinking a passenger liner. He believed the German government must offer compensation. *Volksblatt und Freiheits Freund* felt Wilson had failed to see the other side of the argument. It viewed England, not Germany, as responsible for the attack. Because the ship was carrying weapons, it was a fair target. The paper wondered where American neutrality was when England was setting up a blockade of Germany. And furthermore, it contended that Americans themselves bore some responsibility for the incident. Without American weapons, Germany might have prevailed before the sinking was necessary.

Another incident that drove the United States closer to war with Germany and the *Volksblatt und Freiheits Freund* discussed in depth was the Zimmerman Telegram of 1917. The paper emphasized that the idea that Germany would actively court Mexico seemed ridiculous. It saw it as a clearly fake document produced by the British to draw America into the conflict. However, on March 3, 1917, everything changed. Zimmerman admitted to sending the telegram. The next day, *Volksblatt und Freiheits Freund* began to try to rationalize the telegram. It carried an interview with Zimmerman conducted by a British news agency. He asserted that Germany's actions were just because the United States looked as though it was being pushed closer and closer to war. America, after all, was never the picture of neutrality. The German government had to act in its own defense and court allies where it could. In a later article, "Tit for Tat," *Volksblatt und Freiheits Freund* echoed Zimmerman's sentiments. It reported that America had been responsible for similar plots and American neutrality was a joke.

When not combatting British propaganda, the German American community in Pittsburgh attempted to fulfill Bloedel's other commandment. It, through the Alliance, sought to come to the aid of some of its kinfolk affected by the war. Drives were held, asking people to donate to German widows and orphans as well as the German Red Cross. In 1915, *Volksblatt und Freiheits Freund* urged its readership to donate: "Whoever feels for Mother Germany, whoever is proud of his German blood should help to increase the relief fund…If we can't offer our blood for the good cause, then we can evidence our readiness to give with our money. Everyone do what he can." As a testament to their wealth and devotion, Pittsburgh's German Americans responded quickly and readily. From August 12, 1914, to November 13, 1916, a total of $115,379.97 was donated to the cause. This good-faith charity effort to relieve the suffering of both the German people and German prisoners of war held in Siberia was later seen as more proof of the Alliance's animosity toward the United States. After all, relief efforts continued after the United States cut off diplomatic relations with Germany.

As pro-German and anti-British as the German American community had been prior to America's involvement, everything changed the moment it became clear that the United States was to enter the war. Although the idea of war with the fatherland was indeed heartbreaking, they were first and foremost loyal Americans. *Volksblatt und Freiheits Freund*, along with many German American newspapers, nationally published what it considered a good summation of where it thought German American loyalties lay. It explained that while Germany was still seen as the German American community's mother, the United States was viewed as its wife. Although German Americans' primary loyalty was to their chosen homeland, they could not forget the loyalty owed to Germany. There was also a great fear on the part of many German Americans. After all, they did not know what the nativist, prowar element in Pittsburgh was going to do. They rightly feared becoming targets of violence or intimidation.

These fears were expressed by *Volksblatt und Freiheits Freund*'s April 7, 1917 article entitled "Silence is Golden." They reminded their readers that "no German who obeys the law has anything to fear" and advised them to "hold your tongue and play along." Many members of the non-German community in Pittsburgh did their best to ease the minds of German

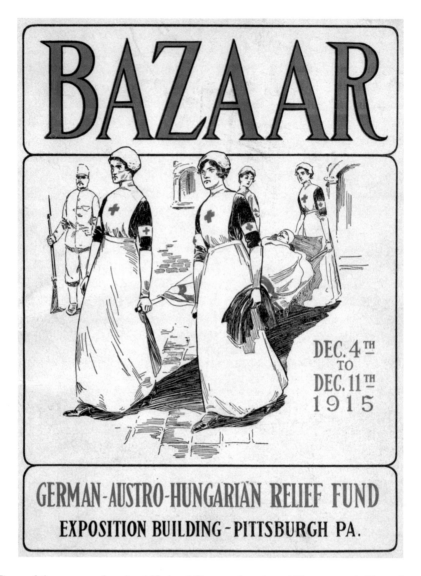

Cover of the program for a local National German American Alliance event held to raise money for German relief, December 1915. *Courtesy of the Heinz History Center.*

Americans. Days earlier, on April 1, the prowar Anglo-American newspaper the *Pittsburg Press* reported on the mass prowar, pro-America meeting held at the Exposition Hall. Although the well-attended meeting was to express support for President Wilson and America's entrance into the war, the *Pittsburg Press* pointed out that there were many German Americans who not only attended but also were asked to be on stage. It reported that the speakers' declarations "were that America is not turning to a war on the German people, but on the Prussian militarism, or as one speaker described it, kaiserism, which is running Germany and is responsible for the outrages driving the United States to war." Both the *Pittsburg Press* and the organizers of the meeting sought to demonstrate both to nativist elements and German Americans still hoping for American neutrality that there was broad support for the war among the entire community.

For their part, many German Americans were also quick to buy Liberty Bonds, including those in the Alliance. In late October 1917, the Alliance appropriated $1,000 from its membership fund in order to buy bonds. Over 1,300 members bought Liberty Bonds on their own, totaling over $270,000 on the bonds. During the second Liberty Loan campaign, over 1,400 of the Alliance's members spent over $223,000 on them. These numbers are amazing, especially considering that they did not raise as much for German war relief. Bonds were bought both out of a sense of patriotic duty as well as proof to the nativist element that they were patriotic Americans.

Although non-Germans were often on the lookout for any signs of un-American behavior, German organizations and social clubs were not disbanded. *Volksblatt und Freiheits Freund* survived for almost twenty-five years after the war was over. That is not to say that certain German organizations did not disappear because of the war. (The Germania Savings Bank was renamed the Citizens Savings Bank of Pittsburgh, for example.) However, the backlash against German immigrants was much less pronounced than in other cities.

The eventual fate of the Alliance is also symptomatic of a national trend to discredit and disband German organizations. At best, it was accused of delaying and discouraging assimilation, and at worst, it was seen as an organ of the German government. Regardless, the U.S. Senate began investigating the group in 1918 when Utah senator William King declared the Alliance to be a threat to America's well being and introduced a bill meant to revoke the Alliance's charter. The Senate investigation lasted from February until April 1918. At issue was the Alliance's involvement in politics, which was something that the national charter strictly forbade. The Alliance argued that most political involvement was done at state and local levels and that local charters did not ban political work. E. Lowry Humes, the U.S. district attorney for western Pennsylvania who investigated the local branch of the Alliance, proved to be a star witness at the Senate hearings. His evidence that the branch was political, had raised money for German war relief and had campaigned against Wilson was enough to condemn it. On April 11, 1918, rather than wait for Congress to revoke the Alliance's charter, it voted to disband.

Nationwide, 60 percent of the German newspapers in the United States had closed before the end of the war. Yet *Volksblatt und Freiheits Freund* survived. While the government and others watched Pittsburgh's German Americans for any signs of disloyalty and there were incidents of violence, the German community itself was not persecuted on a mass scale. Americanization was allowed to happen more gradually, influenced as much by other factors as the war itself. Ten years after the war, when the *Audit of International Institute Material on Pittsburgh's Nationality Community* was conducted, the authors stated, "We are not ordinarily conscious of their origin, i.e., a name with German spelling is quite commonly thought of as a plain American name."

While there were hundreds of German American organizations in Pittsburgh, I have chosen to discuss how three of them—the German Evangelical Church, the Knights of St. George and the German Beneficial Union—dealt with the challenges the war brought with it.

Pittsburgh's German Evangelical Church (now Smithfield United Church of Christ) is the oldest church in Pittsburgh. In 1782, the initial forty-two church members began meeting in a log cabin (presumably along with their wives and children, who were not allowed to be members). By the time the Great War engulfed Europe, it was one of the pillars of Pittsburgh's German community. The church had already moved to Smithfield Street and built a German business district on church-owned property. Services were held in German, and parish records were written in German.

However, by 1917, the character of the church was already changing. Its parishioners were moving to the suburbs, and the characters of those who were left were becoming Americanized. The young people in the community were second- and third-generation German Americans and were taught English in public schools, regardless of what their parents spoke at home. They valued being American and often married people who were not German. They did not want to attend a service they could not understand. In addition, there was incredible pressure to be American. According to the book *German Evangelical Protestant Smithfield Church Congregational History*, "The war was directed primarily against Germany but the war hysteria frequently included everything in its attacks that had any relationship with Germany, past or present." As a result, the church introduced bilingual morning services. The pastor would give a sermon in German and an address in English one week, and the next week switch the order. This new effort to be bilingual

German business district on Smithfield Street in 1914. The land was owned and rented out by the German Evangelical Church (far right). *Courtesy of the Smithfield United Church of Christ.*

did not extend to the church records. English translations were not included until after the war. In this way, the church sought to preserve its heritage while at the same time, attempted to demonstrate that its congregation was composed of loyal Americans willing to change.

Any suggestion of pro-German sympathies, real or imagined, could have turned the Anglo-American community against the church. However, the church's pastor at the time, Reverend Dr. Carl A. Voss, was not going to let that happen. Voss urged his parishioners to be patriotic Americans. The church claimed membership of 121 young men who served in the armed forces, of whom 5 did not come home. The women of the community were active in Red Cross work, so much so that they earned the commendation of the local, state and national authorities. The parishioners, as well as the church itself, purchased Liberty and Victory Bonds, totaling over a $500,000.

In August 1918, the church had a flag-dedication ceremony. As he presented a flag to Voss, the president of the congregation, W.H. Schove, said, "In the name of this congregation I present this American flag in the hope that [as] it hangs above the altar it may ennoble our hearts with loyalty and enkindle our souls with patriotism." The Red Cross auxiliary members,

German Evangelical Church's Red Cross workers. *Courtesy of the Smithfield United Church of Christ.*

A group of Knights of St. George cadets about 1916. *Courtesy of the Diocese of Pittsburgh Archives.*

as well as some of the community's children, presented Voss with a Red Cross flag as well. Both were displayed above the altar.

Because of the church's efforts, the Pittsburgh community embraced it. It and its pastor were well regarded. However, the war took its toll. After the war, being known as German was less and less appealing. In the 1920s, the parish records, which were once written solely in German, had English translations pasted next to them. Eventually, the records were written in English with German translations before the German disappeared entirely. As the congregation changed, so did its name, eventually becoming the Smithfield United Church of Christ. The Knights of St. George, a Roman Catholic, German beneficial union would approach the war in a similar way to the German Evangelical Church.

The Knights of St. George was founded in Pittsburgh in 1880 by German Catholics in Pittsburgh and Allegheny City. It not only provided its members with insurance but was also a social organization. One of the unusual aspects of the society was the Knights of St. George cadets. Beginning in 1914, boys aged twelve and up could join. These boys wore uniforms and were drilled weekly according to United States' Army Infantry Drill Regulations. The organization was also a social one for the boys. Business and professional men would come and give talks and demonstrations. Upon reaching the age of sixteen, they were initiated into the Order of the Knights of St. George.

The newsletter for the Knights of St. George was published in German for the most part until after the United States entered the war. The first issue completely in English was published in August 1918. The next month, it announced the creation of a war fund. Every member was expected to contribute another a quarter a month, which would go into the war fund and help the union deal with the "abnormal condition and state of affairs in the industrial, political, social, and economic life of our country." The Knights of St. George also stated that over two thousand of its members were involved in the war and 10 percent of its membership was eligible for the draft. Some of its members had already died fighting in the war, and the extra quarter was to help offset the cost of paying on the insurance of those affected by the war. The newsletter continues that only, "Almighty God alone knows just how many of our Brothers will fall in battle and be sacrificed to the God of war and on the altar of Freedom and Liberty."

The September 1918 newsletter continued to outline what the Knights of St. George considered the duty for all loyal Americans. It asked its readers:

Are you cooperating with the Food Administration because you have to or because you want to? Do you call yourself a loyal American citizen, anxious for the speedy triumph of the American cause, the success of its brave soldiers abroad, and the welfare of its fine people at home and yet dare to hold back and whine and quibble and say you can't or you don't want to, or you must now know the reason why, when you are called to conform to requirements? Are you only willing to follow orders because it suites your convenience…Or are you man enough to say: That which is best for my country is best for me. I will follow the call of my trade; serve as it demanded of me; do what is required; stand fast for the good of the whole regardless of my own apparent interests…On your answers to such questions as these will depend your status in this country now, in the time of action, when each man's help is needed, later in the time of judgment, when each man's record is reviewed. In God's name stand up.

The Knights of St. George proved its loyalty to America by challenging its members to be the best Americans they could be and support their country without complaint. In October, it pointed out that being members of a fraternal organization already made its members used to the ideas of thrift and less-extravagant living. Throughout the duration of the war it also reported on what local German Catholic churches were doing as a part of the war effort.

It's war fund continued after the signing of the armistice to provide for the men who came home and the families of those who did not. In November 1918, having proved itself as a loyal American institution, it began publishing some articles in German again without preamble or explanation. It lasted until 1983 when it merged with another fraternal union, the William Penn Association. The German Beneficial Union, however, approached the war in a much different way than the German Evangelical Church and the Knights of St. George.

The German Beneficial Union (now the Greater Beneficial Union of Pittsburgh or GBU) was founded in 1892 by Louis Volz, August Wedemeyer, Louis Thumm, Henry Graf and Julius Eicher. It was their hope that GBU would benefit the large number of working-class German Americans in Allegheny County and add to their prestige in the community. According to the company's history, GBU was intended to be a "mutual benefit association and life insurance company, a vehicle for ethnic identity, and multiethnic cooperation, a close-knit neighborhood club and community social center, a workingmen's club, and social group for the elderly, a provider of a loan

The U.S. Food Administration encouraged thrift through advertisements such as this one. It was published in local papers, including the Knights of St. George newsletter. *Courtesy of the Library of Congress.*

Fraternity

IS THE KEYSTONE OF THE GRAND ARCH OF MODERN PROGRESS AND CIVILIZATION.

After reading this Pamphlet thoroughly you are respectfully requested to join our Union. If you are well-to-do, your name will be a support to the Union. If you are not well-to-do the Union will be a support to you.

——o——

„Spare in der Zeit, so haft Du in der Not."

Nachdem Sie den Inhalt dieses Büchleins genau gelesen, entschließen Sie sich, dem Bunde als Mitglied beizutreten. Sind Sie reich oder wohlhabend, so bildet Ihr Name eine Stütze für den Bund; sind Sie arm, so bildet der Bund eine Stütze für Sie.

 5

Left and Opposite: This GBU pamphlet from 1922 demonstrates that after the war, the company felt free to return to using German freely. *Courtesy of Dr. Michael Shaughnessy.*

when no other financial institution would grant one, and a significant charitable contributor." The founders had hoped that because of its social aspect, GBU would also help promote a united German American identity. However, GBU's founders also realized that they were running a business. At no point in its history was its membership restricted by ethnicity, religion or gender. The only qualifications for membership, which were listed in the first issue of its publication, the *Union Reporter*, was that the person be of good moral character. The newsletter included articles in both English and German, particularly when it discussed policy. This helped attract second- and third-generation German Americans to the union.

When war broke out in Europe, GBU was not only an important organization in the German American community but also staunchly pro-German. The *Union Reporter* published many letters and articles in support of the German cause until mid-1915, when it instead focused on advocating neutrality. The September 1915 issues of the newsletter carried in it a

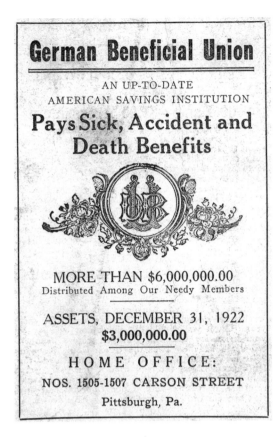

German Beneficial Union

AN UP-TO-DATE
AMERICAN SAVINGS INSTITUTION

Pays Sick, Accident and Death Benefits

MORE THAN $6,000,000.00
Distributed Among Our Needy Members

ASSETS, DECEMBER 31, 1922
$3,000,000.00

HOME OFFICE:
NOS. 1505-1507 CARSON STREET
Pittsburgh, Pa.

petition from the twenty-three thousand members of GBU and signed by founder Volz to stop the sale of weapons to the Allies. Surprisingly, GBU leaders continued to encourage American neutrality through 1917, even after America entered the war. However, in January 1918, it was made extremely clear that the organization stood firmly behind the U.S. government and its actions. GBU leaders encouraged its members to buy Liberty Bonds and Postal Savings Stamps and to donate to the American Red Cross. (They also noted that the federal government was to be sent a complete list of each district's donations.)

In February, Volz noted that "there are no German-Americans[,] we are all Americans" when he announced that GBU would contribute to the War Savings Stamp campaign. In July, the leadership of the GBU thought it prudent to drop German from its name. It was simply the Beneficial Union (BU) until the 1920s. (The Second World War caused the company to change its name to the Greater Beneficial Union, which it still uses today.) For the most part, however, it was business as usual for GBU during the war. The only accusations that seem to have been levied against the federal government by GBU was at the Carrick district lodge, which was under surveillance for the duration of the war. Despite this, membership in the organization grew. Between 1914 and 1918, it increased from twenty-two thousand to more than thirty-three thousand members.

CHAPTER FIVE

PITTSBURGH'S UNIVERSITIES

Duquesne University of the Holy Ghost (most commonly called Duquesne University), the University of Pittsburgh and Carnegie Institute of Technology (now Carnegie Mellon University), Pittsburgh's three largest colleges, were affected by the Great War and contributed to the war effort in a number of ways. However, each of them approached the challenges of the war differently. These three colleges were chosen because in addition to their size, they also included groups of student soldiers.

Duquesne University was founded in 1878 by an order of Roman Catholic priests, the Holy Ghost Fathers (also known as the Spiritans). Although the Spiritans were founded in France in 1703, the order was also extremely active in Germany. It was German Spiritans—led by Joseph Strub, C.S.Sp.— who, after being expelled from Germany by German chancellor Otto von Bismarck, eventually settled in Pittsburgh and founded Pittsburgh Catholic College (which would later be renamed Duquesne University). German and Irish Spiritans formed some of the college's first instructors and presidents, giving it a very strong ethnic identity catering to the children of Pittsburgh's Catholic immigrants.

When World War I broke out in Europe thirty years later, Duquesne University had not completely shed the German aspects of its identity. It was not, however, considered a German institution. For example, the university appears to have refrained from any debate over American neutrality, which plagued other institutions. The *Duquesne Monthly*, the student newspaper, ran only a few articles that discussed the issue. Only one article, published in

America Must Win

Every American Must Help

ENLIST
IF YOU
CAN

PLANT A GARDEN
SAVE
FOOD

BUY
LIBERTY
BONDS and W. S. S.

WORK
FOR THE
RED CROSS

Duquesne University Is Doing All This

There Are 345 Stars in Her Service Flag
BUT WATCH THE TOTAL GO UP!

6

Advertisement in Duquesne University's theater program, 1918. *Courtesy of Duquesne University.*

February 1915, and written by student Edward Nemmer openly advocates American neutrality. The article is about the celebrations taking place marking the centennial of the last battle between America and England. The article makes it clear that America should value peace and not get involved in a war that is not its to fight. Nemmer reminds his readers that taking sides in the war causes jealousy. And alliances and jealousy, according to Nemmer, are what caused the war and accelerated it to the point where it practically engulfed the entire continent of Europe. He concludes by praising Wilson's dedication to neutrality.

However, when America chose to enter into Europe's war, Duquesne University made it very clear from the beginning that it stood firmly behind its country. As senior John J. McDonough expressed in his *Duquesne Monthly* editorial in May 1917, "Having unsheathed the sword, it is our duty to stand by the sword. And with every desire for peace we must nevertheless...stand loyally by the nation in every trial." Shortly after the declaration of war, Duquesne University president Reverend Martin Hehir, C.S.Sp., presided over a flag-raising ceremony, telling his students that "there are or should be, gentlemen, two great loves in the soul of man—the love of God and the love of country...I believe that the more a man loves God, the more genuine, the more disinterested, the more self-sacrificing, is his love of country."

Hehir and his university soon proved that they were willing to back up his words with proof of their love of country. A program of military training, which included instruction about the Constitution and the federal government, was instituted in the summer of 1917. By the fall, one hundred guns were purchased for four dollars apiece, and two infantry companies were organized at the university. They performed exercises and drills on campus. This was part of a greater nationwide effort. As a part of the Draft Law of 1917, all male college students had to undergo military training.

On February 26, 1918, Duquesne University blessed a service flag and raised it in honor of the more than two hundred men who had joined the armed services. In and among other items about the war service of Duquesne men, the *Duquesne Monthly* published the names of those students and alumni killed in action. A total of fifteen would not come home: seven were killed in action, and another eight died from disease.

A Students Army Training Corps unit (SATC) was established on campus in the fall of 1918. Lack of space forced the School of Social Services, founded in 1916, to be discontinued in order to house it. The college housed 175 men (including some high school boys) in the campus theater. They drilled on campus and instructed in the art of war in the Vandergrift

Duquesne University's SATC united in front of the Administration Building, December 1918. *Courtesy of Duquesne University.*

Building in downtown Pittsburgh. (Eventually, when they outgrew the barracks space on campus, some of the students would be housed in the lyceum at nearby Epiphany Church.) These students were divided into two infantry companies and drilled Monday and Thursday evenings, supervised by three army captains and one colonel. Their classes were adjusted so that they could be of the most value militarily. After the war, the SATC would be replaced by the Reserve Officer Training Corps (ROTC).

Duquesne University also showed its patriotism and pride in various other ways. German Spiritan priests who serviced the local German churches officially stopped preaching in German. The school song, written by Father Mallory in 1912, was also discarded because it had been set to the tune of the German national anthem. Despite the climate, Duquesne University saw no reason to stop teaching German. German-language classes were offered throughout the duration of the war.

Carnegie Technical School was founded in 1900 by Scottish-born steel tycoon Andrew Carnegie. He was highly unimpressed with the liberal arts institutions of the Pittsburgh area and wanted to create a free technical school where young Pittsburgh men and women could be prepared for careers in Pittsburgh's industries. It offered two-year certificates and four-year degrees and was composed of four schools: the School of Science and

Technology, the School of Fine and Applied Arts, the School for Apprentices and Journeymen and the Margaret Morrison Carnegie School for Women. Although originally intended to be free, that ideal proved unfeasible, and a small tuition was charged. In 1908, tuition was fifty dollars, but it had been raised to seventy-five dollars by 1918. By 1912, the school underwent the first of many name changes and became the Carnegie Institute of Technology (known as Carnegie Tech).

When it became clear that American entrance into the war was inevitable, the young school was eager to prove itself ready. Thirteen days before war was declared, Carnegie Tech's trustees placed all of its services and equipment at the government's disposal. Soon, the campus was buzzing with young male students who were taking part in voluntary drills. In November, the first group of draftees arrived onto campus for training. Before the end of the war, eight thousand young men trained, lived and studied either on campus or nearby. Each was trained in one of seventeen classifications set out by the U.S. Army, which included everything from mechanics to musicians to propeller makers.

Not underestimating the role women in Pittsburgh could play during the war, Margaret Morrison Carnegie School for Women offered specialized classes in stenography and other subjects that could be of use. Concerns for the welfare of the female student population during the war were also taken into account. Disturbed by reports that the soldiers' presence on campus had attracted a number of "undesirable women," Dean Mary Bidwell Breed asked the college's president to forbid soldiers to come onto the women's college's grounds. She hoped to protect her students from inappropriate advances. Strict curfews were also in place for the women's dorms, and no man was allowed to enter them.

The Carnegie Tech branch of the ROTC was in full swing by early 1918. From July until September, exercises were held in Schenley Oval. By October 1918, Carnegie Tech was to get its own SATC unit. In order to make that a reality, all classes except those related to the war were to be halted. However, this never occurred because Washington kept changing the orders, and the flu epidemic hit full swing in Pittsburgh.

Another feature that was added to campus was one that was extremely crucial to the school's ability to keep its doors open during the winter months. In 1917, the United States was experiencing a horrific fuel crisis. Most homes and businesses were heated using natural gas instead of coal, and there was soon a shortage of both. Ration measures were enacted, and in some areas, natural gas could only be delivered by those who had licenses. Carnegie Tech was extremely affected by this gas crisis. One of the city's leading natural gas suppliers, Peoples Gas, notified the school that rates for gas would increase and that there was probably going to be a shortage of gas that winter.

Since the school was nearly wholly dependent on gas, a solution needed to be found. In the summer of 1917, Carnegie Tech began exploring the possibility that they could provide their own gas by drilling on campus. Even though other regional gas wells were drying up, engineers and geologists believed that gas did exist under the campus. In July, the trustees approved the $10,000 plan to keep the school open. West Virginia's state geologist I.C. White identified a good location for the well. It was supposed to be able to last the school for four years, and when it went dry, they planned to sell it to help recoup some of the cost.

Board members worked to keep the cost of the well down. Taylor Allderdice managed to purchase the casing at cost. The Carnegie Natural Gas Co. provided free equipment, and oil- and gas-well contractors Barnhart and McCall did the work at cost. The plan worked. Gas was found. Although it was not enough to cover all the college's needs, it helped alleviate the problem. The line was connected with Peoples Gas Company lines in order to supplement as needed. Plans were put in place to drill deeper if needed; however, their supplies saw them through the war. Carnegie Tech's efforts were not in vain. A commission sent by the War Department said, "Tech has exceptionally fine equipment and a great advantage over other schools in this country in that respect."

The Pittsburgh Academy (now known as the University of Pittsburgh) was granted its charter in 1787, although classes did not begin for another two years. It was founded by Scottish-born Hugh Henry Brackenridge. Although its first building was located in downtown Pittsburgh, it had made the move into Oakland by the early 1900s, when it changed its name to the University of Pittsburgh.

The University of Pittsburgh was perhaps the most prepared out of the three colleges discussed for America's entry into the Great War. The day after the United States declared war on Germany, the School of Medicine unveiled a field hospital that was ready for service. The field hospital was the work of a small, dedicated number of wealthier Americans who began preparations shortly after Europe erupted in war. They opposed Wilson's dedication to neutrality and were sure that, sooner or later, the United States would become involved in the Allies' struggle. They wanted to be prepared for that eventuality. They began training their own officer corps and used private funding to establish a camp in Plattsburg, New York.

The Plattsburg camp was taken on by the dean of the School of Medicine at the time, Dr. Thomas S. Arbuthnot, and senior professor of medicine Dr. James D. Heard. Together, they raised the necessary $75,000 in private funds; bought a building; enlisted and trained surgeons, nurses and orderlies; and equipped a complete unit (which would become AEF Base Hospital 27). Because of the hard work and preparation that had gone into it before America entered the war, it arrived in Angers, France, before American troops did. While it arrived in France with only five hundred beds, by the time the armistice was signed, that number had grown to five thousand. Out of the over 19,000 men that the base hospital treated before the war, only 277 died. The University of Pittsburgh's medical school contributed to the war effort in other ways also. Out of the one hundred faculty members who enlisted in the war, fifty-eight were from the medical school.

Similar to Duquesne University and Carnegie Tech, male students at the University of Pittsburgh also needed to take part in military training. Six days a week, faculty members with National Guard experience conducted one-hour drills for the university's students. These drills were done without uniforms or weapons as uniforms weren't issued to students until May 1918.

The University of Pittsburgh also made the unusual decision to dismiss all its faculty pro forma until a decision could be reached as to what classes were to remain for the duration of the war. Some classes did remain, although the focus was placed on classes that had military uses. Within six months, the university had classes filled with more than two thousand men.

Female students were also engaged in war work, including knitting, making surgical dressing, scrapbooking for the soldiers at war and fashioning service flags. Some also insisted in participating alongside their male counterparts in close-order drills. The campus was also buzzing with local celebrities as part of drives to sell Liberty Bonds.

New buildings were also built in order to accommodate the soldiers and students on and around the University of Pittsburgh's campus. On O'Hara Street, army barracks, a mess hall, an administrative building and a YMCA hospitality house were built. Housing soldiers was a big issue facing the

Opposite, top: The University of Pittsburgh's Base Hospital 27 in Angers, France. *Courtesy of the Heinz History Center.*

Opposite, bottom: Plans for the University of Pittsburgh's Base Hospital 27 in Angers, France. *Courtesy of the Heinz History Center.*

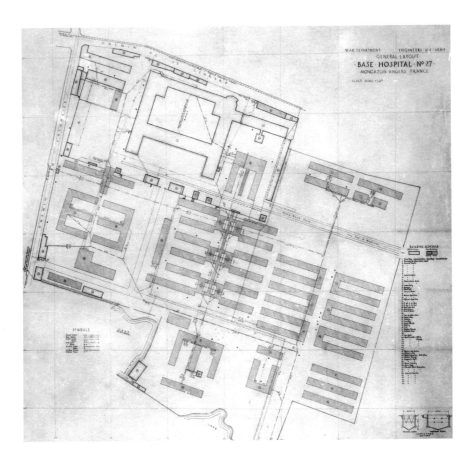

college. While some were housed in barracks, others were housed in an office building, a fraternity house, the Logan Armory and even Soldiers and Sailors Memorial Hall.

In September 1918, University of Pittsburgh chancellor Samuel McCormick called a meeting in Plattsburgh of all the college presidents to inform them that the government was taking over the training of officers in the SATC. The SATC was split into two sections. Section A was composed of those who were to be trained as officers. Section B was made up of students being trained in technical courses.

When the October 1918 influenza outbreak occurred in Pittsburgh, the campus was quarantined. Classes were stopped abruptly as a preventive measure, although outdoor drills were permitted. Only four football games were played. Although the quarantine only lasted forty days, by the time it was lifted, the war was over. The SATC was disbanded on November 26, 1918, and by December 21, all the soldier-students were out of the service. By the war's end, 5,000 students had been members of the SATC. In addition, 167 faculty members, 930 students and over 1,400 alumni had seen military service. As life returned to normal, the university made the decision to fit a full years' worth of classes into six months so none of its students fell behind.

Chapter Six

Pittsburghers at War

War is not two great armies meeting in the clash and frenzy of battle. War is a boy carried on a stretcher looking up at God's blue sky with bewildered eyes that are soon to close; war is a woman carrying a child that has been injured by a shell," Pittsburgh mystery author Mary Roberts Rinehart wrote in 1915. She spoke with authority on the matter—she had seen it first hand. Rinehart was a thirty-eight-year-old wife and mother when war broke out. She was already a well-known fiction author (she would later be called the American Agatha Christie despite Rinehart's earlier start) frequently published in the *Saturday Evening Post*.

Rinehart was on vacation in Canada with her husband and sons in the summer of 1914 when they received the news that war erupted in Europe. That night she resolved to go to the war zone. The *Saturday Evening Post* was thrilled with the idea of sending one of its best writers to war, promising her $1,000 for each article she wrote. However, Dr. Stan Rinehart, Mary's husband, was not thrilled with the idea of his wife's putting herself in danger and forbade her from going. He would eventually relent, and Mary left for London in January 1915.

Arriving in London as a war correspondent did not guarantee passage to the war zone. There was a ban on correspondents at the front, and London was buzzing with hundreds of people in Rinehart's position. Mary, however, managed to secure a meeting with the head of the Belgian Red Cross (who was also the personal physician to Queen Elisabeth of Belgium). She convinced him that since she was a trained nurse, she could

Mary Rinehart. *Courtesy of the Heinz History Center.*

describe hospitals in the war zone to American readers more accurately than her male counterparts. It worked, and she soon found herself on her way to Belgium.

Mary received her first taste of war before reaching Belgium. While she was in Dunkirk, France, at dinner, the Germans began to bomb the city. When she asked the maître d' where she should go, he told her she was safe, but she could go to the cellar if it made her feel better. While she desperately wanted to seek safety in the cellars, she knew that she could not. Mary later explained, "I felt that, as the only woman and the only American about, I held the reputation of America and my sex in my hands." Since the officers she was dining with did not seek refuge, she could not either. The bombing continued until 3:00 a.m.

When she arrived in Belgium, she saw the devastation of war firsthand, even becoming the first female correspondent to be taken into no man's land between the Allied and German lines. This was a terrifying trek for Mary. Although it was late at night, she was dressed in khaki and felt that she was an easy target in the moonlight. The men accompanying her offered to take her back to the relative safety of the Allied lines. She refused and continued along with the male correspondents and their entourage of guards until they were within two hundred yards of the German lines.

Mary accomplished a number of firsts during her time in Europe: the first reporter to interview King Albert of Belgium about the war, the first American to interview Queen Mary of England and the first woman behind British lines. She also interviewed Winston Churchill and French General Foch. Foch, in particular, hoped that she could combat German propaganda in America. Although she had gone to Europe with the intention of writing articles that kept America away from war, she returned with a sense that entering into the Great War was her country's moral duty. Her war articles, published shortly after her return, made her a celebrity and in prime position to exalt the American government's cause in 1917.

She wrote "The Altar of Freedom" for the *Saturday Evening Post* in late April 1917. She told Americans, "Because I am a woman I cannot die for my country, but I am doing a far harder thing. I am giving a son to the service of his country." Her oldest, Stan Jr., was already a member of the ROTC at Harvard and did go to France. Her husband, too, would enlist as a doctor (although he was destined to remain stateside). The War Department used Mary as a propagandist; she traveled, spoke and wrote articles about American preparedness. Although mothers and wives of troops were not permitted to go to France as nurses, Mary did eventually return to

Europe with the Red Cross. She arrived days before the armistice was signed and was still in Paris when it was announced.

"The Altar of Freedom" and Mary's other war articles undoubtedly helped ease the pain of many Pittsburgh mothers who were preparing to send their sons to war, of whom there were many, because when the United States entered the war, Pittsburgh men did not hesitate to answer their government's call for troops. The adjunct general of the commonwealth of Pennsylvania estimated that sixty thousand men from Pittsburgh and Allegheny County answered the government's call and entered the service. Over one thousand of those men did not return. They came from every walk of life. Some, such as William and Alexander Thaw, were among Pittsburgh's wealthiest and most elite citizens. Others, such as Thomas Enright, came from a working-class background. While some fought because they were drafted, many others joined out of a sense of patriotism and the feeling that this was a fight that America could not afford to lose. There was a feeling that democracy itself rested upon their shoulders. Romanticism of war, the excitement of battle and a deep desire to take part in their generation's one great war caused many Pittsburghers to flock to the registration booths.

Soldiers such as Private Philip J. Pricer of Bloomfield enlisted out of love not only for country but also for family. The forty-two-year-old who worked in Carnegie Steel's shipping department was so concerned that his brother, who was in poor health, would be drafted early that he enlisted in July 1917, hoping that a family member's service would deter his brother's being drafted. However, Philip never made it home. He was killed in action on July 7, 1918, leaving behind two brothers, three sisters and a father.

Some able-bodied men considered it shameful to stay at home, even if they had dependents (a legitimate reason for deferring the draft). For example, one man had a wife, four children, two parents, a mother-in-law and two sisters depending on him and his income. On his registration card, when asked if he wished exemption, he responded, "My God. No." While another family man responded, "I think I am worthy of it, but I don't approve." Women, too, were anxious to swell the ranks of war nurses in Europe. Pittsburgh lost some of its most qualified nurses to the cause and had to rush to train more when the city was in need of them.

Local newspapers even became part of the government recruitment effort, encouraging young men to enlist by publishing highly censored prowar letters from local soldiers. Former Northside policeman John Conley's letter to his brother excitedly described getting the best of the "Huns," who were coming at them with "liquid fire guns." According to the letter, the

Soldiers marching down Smithfield Street in downtown Pittsburgh. *Courtesy of the Heinz History Center.*

Pittsburghers giving their soldiers a proper send off at the B&O Railroad Station, September 23, 1917. *Courtesy of the Heinz History Center.*

Michael Musmanno, born in McKees Rocks in 1897, joined the
American Army in World War I. Although he never saw action during
that war, he became a famous Pittsburgh judge, eventually winning a
Purple Heart during World War II and serving on the Pennsylvania
Supreme Court. His uniform is that of a typical doughboy. *Courtesy of
the Duquesne University Archives.*

American troops received a warning about the attack and were prepared. As the Germans charged them, one of their men jumped up on the parapet and called for a volley. "The Huns got it, and got it fair and square. Those that we didn't mow down became confused and turned the liquid fire upon their own troops. Gosh, but it was funny and we all laughed so much that we only bagged about half as much as we ought to have." He concluded his letter by telling his brother to "C'mover." In another published letter, Sargent Thomas J. Cavanaugh, a former Mount Washington police officer, wrote to his old co-worker James W. Eagan. In his letter, he admitted that while they lost some good men in the fighting, the casualty list was not as high as it should have been. In describing the mood of the captured German soldiers, he wrote, "These prisoners are nearly always glad to be captured. This is especially true of the younger elements of the German soldiers, whose ages are from fifteen upward. However, once and awhile [*sic*] you get an old lead who prefers to die fighting."

Also, soldiers' visits home were cause for celebration in local newspapers. For example, when Lieutenants Cedric Benz and John Shenkel came home on furlough in August 1918, the papers were chomping at the bit to report on their every move. They were two of the heroes of the Battle of Hill 204. The Battle of Hill 204 was part of the larger Battle of Chateau-Thierry. For many of the local doughboys, it was their first taste of action. The Germans had taken the high ground and were raining down heavy machine-gun fire on the Allied troops trapped in their trenches. The machine guns were decimating the Allied troops, and the French general in command concluded that they needed to be taken out. He was, however, reluctant to order any of his men into the "inferno of heated lead." Instead, he asked for volunteers. Lieutenants Benz and Shenkel quickly volunteered to lead men into the hail of gunfire. Many other Pittsburghers followed them, and a French officer led the third group made of Frenchmen.

When the order came, they charged up over the trenches to cheers. Benz later recalled, "Lordy how those Yankee boys—under fire for the first time—did cheer! Made a fellow feel proud to be with him and made him feel as though he could take on the whole world single-handed. And we went over, the machine guns got down to work in dead earnest again. Whizz-z-z-z! Whi-r-r-r! came the bullets, but I doubt if any of our fellows heard them. It was just like playing football, you know—get the other fellow or be 'got' yourself." They charged up the hill—Shenkel on one side, Benz (still smoking his pipe) on the other—and the French in the middle before the Germans knew they were coming.

Above: The back of the Victory Medal distributed to American World War I veterans. It lists the names of the Allied countries. *Courtesy of the Duquesne University Archives.*

Left: The front of the Victory Medal distributed to American World War I veterans. *Courtesy of the Duquesne University Archives.*

Once they reached the Germans, Benz said, "Some of my men seemed to have forgotten what their guns were for, instead of using them to shoot with, they turned them into clubs and in this manner forced the boche [Germans] back and back and back. Some of the Yanks used their fists with telling effects." The maneuver was a success; they managed to kill or capture over a hundred Germans. Benz and Shenkel were both cited for their bravery, earning the French Croix de Guerre and the American Distinguished Service Cross.

When Shenkel and Benz returned to Pittsburgh, they were not only hounded by the press to tell their story but also asked to speak at a number of meetings. A part of the job for a soldier while home on leave was to use the attention to garner further support for the war. For example, at a meeting of women, Benz assured them that regardless what they'd heard about the horrors of war, "the American soldier dies with a smile and he says to those around him, 'Go get 'em boys.'"

Pittsburghers were also instrumental in establishing the 351st Field Artillery as a strong African American fighting force with strong ties to the Pittsburgh community. Understand that the U.S. Army never intended for African Americans from Pittsburgh to serve in the 351st. On October 31, 1917, a second contingent of African American men from Pittsburgh arrived at Camp Lee, Virginia, to half-finished, windowless barracks. Like the group that arrived a week before them, they soon discovered that they were members of the 504th and 505th Service Battalions. They would not be armed; they would not fight. When they finally left for France, they would be deployed one mile from the fighting to dig trenches and do other support work. There was also no opportunity to advance. All of their officers would be white, and the most they could hope for was to rise to first-class private. As Reverend Shelton Hale, Pittsburgh pastor at the Church of the Holy Cross, wrote in 1942, "They all went away with high hopes of serving their country with dignity and honor. They soon found themselves in overhauls with picks and shovels…Negroes were expected to be stevedores and were expected to do the trench digging, unloading, etc., in Europe."

This did not sit well with the men. Most of them had at least a high school diploma, and several were college educated. Nine of them banded together to fight what they saw as injustice and discrimination. After breakfast each morning and after lunch each afternoon, they would slip away from their companies and meet far enough away to not be recognized easily, bringing with them a heavy board, paper, envelops and decks of cards. If they were spotted, they would play cards in order to not arouse suspicion that they were plotting to challenge their plight. Austin Norris, who had a law degree from Yale University, was chosen to be their leader. Each man was required to write two letters to prominent Pittsburghers detailing their treatment. When the letters were finished, the others read them over and made sure no one was writing to the same person. The process took about five days. Once completed, they drew straws to see who would take them into Petersburg, Virginia, to mail them.

Norris drew the short straw, and Ode Hall insisted on going with him. The trip to Petersburg was dangerous. It meant going AWOL for a few days. It also meant court-martial or worse if they were caught with the letters. On the night Hall and Norris left for Petersburg, Norris hid the letters in his pant legs and socks. Although he was planning on returning by the next night, he did not return for two nights. However, his mission was successful. He had secured the help of a doctor in Petersburg, and their letters were on the way to Pittsburgh.

A friend of one of the men said that "hell broke lose" the day the letters reached Pittsburgh. The strong African American community in Pittsburgh was livid, and it enlisted the help of Congressman John Morrin and Postmaster William H. Davis. Reverend Shelton Hale was sent to assess the situation. He carried with him letters guaranteeing the character and training of many of the men, as well as letters of introduction from men in the War Department. He was told by the commanding officers he talked to that nothing could be done. The officer explained that the men were not being discriminated against because there were white stevedores, too.

However, within a few months everything changed. The pressure that Pittsburgh put on the War Department must have worked. Although the protesters could have been court-martialed for their actions, they were instead transferred to Camp Meade and allowed to join the 351st. Upon arrival, to further their disgust, the Pittsburgh men found that other African American soldiers who had less than a third grade education were already there and in the process of learning how to use artillery pieces that required a strong background in mathematics. There was speculation that the army had wanted African American units to fail and had assigned the most ill-suited men to artillery training and the best to support services. However, it is just as likely that the army didn't look at the men's background before assigning them to specific jobs. Men were needed to fill the ranks, and they assigned jobs based on when and where they signed up. Regardless, the Pittsburgh men excelled at Camp Meade in Georgia.

Donald Jefferson, then a University of Pittsburgh pharmacy student in his early twenties, was assigned as a private in the supply company. He soon rose to the rank of regimental supply sergeant. Austin Norris and John Carter Robinson were recommended to the Third Officers' training school. Their education was a factor in the army's decision. Artillerists needed to have excellent reading and math skills.

Because Norris and Robinson were late in being admitted to the school, they had to work twice as hard to catch up. As they were two of very few African Americans in the school, they faced some harsh discrimination from the Southern men, although the Northern students welcomed them. However, when the entire school was quarantined together because of the measles, prejudices lessened, and they all "shared equally in the good and the bad of the school." So much so, that upon graduation, their white classmates who did not think they would come to the diploma ceremony, sent twenty men to make sure they dressed and attended. They gained their commissions in South Carolina, and Robinson believes they were the first two African Americans to do so in American history. Robinson was placed on detachment services and tasked with training new recruits. He excelled at his job and was offered a permanent position. He chose to go overseas

Donald C. Jefferson in uniform. *Courtesy of the Heinz History Center.*

instead. Norris, whose law training made him good at paperwork, was given a desk job sorting out the papers for several companies.

Jefferson would later be sent to a school at Camp Zachary Taylor in Louisville, Kentucky, in order to become an officer. He finished among the top ten out of the two thousand candidates in August 1918. He later recalled that being in uniform and earning his bars did not earn him respect in the Jim Crow South. One example of the discrimination these men faced occurred when Jefferson and other African American artillery officers were riding a train to a camp in South Carolina shortly before shipping off to France. They walked past the "colored" car and went looking for the conductor in order to request Pullman seats. They reached a car reserved for white passengers and were told by an attendant that if they did not leave immediately he would "summon the law." Jefferson later recalled what happened next, "We stood our ground and said we are the law." Having no response, silence fell over the crowded train car as the men were silently led to their seats.

While working on the supply books at Camp Meade, Jefferson was asked by the man in charge of forming the African American artillery regiment, Colonel W.E. Cole, if there were any more men like them in Pittsburgh. When Jefferson answered in the affirmative, he asked the War Department for permission to try to recruit more Pittsburgh men. As a result, hundreds more joined the ranks.

The 351st left for France in June 1918. In France, it underwent more training. Its commanding officer was replaced with Colonel Wade H. Carpenter. Carpenter, in his civilian life, was a Mississippi plantation owner, who told his men, "You are all liars and thieves. But you can't help that. Your ancestors before you, as always, had to steal food and lie for each other to live, avoid punishment or death. It's in your blood and you can't help it." However, by the end of the war, the men had changed his mind. Upon returning to America in 1919, he told them, "I am glad and surprised. You have proved to me that you are not liars and thieves. In all of my military career, I have never met or commanded a finer regiment or more capable one. I am proud of the 351st Field Artillery—every man who belonged to it."

Although the field artillery fought in only a few battles—the war was nearly over by the time it got through with training—its story shows the tenacity of a small group of Pittsburgh men as it struggled to break down racial barriers.

Pittsburgh also provided the war with one of its first American airmen: William Thaw. He wrote in August 1914, shortly after deciding to join the French Foreign Legion, "I am going to take a part, however small, in the

The 351ˢᵗ Field Artillery's homecoming parade. *Courtesy of the Heinz History Center.*

greatest and probably last, war in history, which has apparently developed into a fight of civilization against barbarism." At twenty-one, Thaw, a bit of a free spirit, had already lived somewhat of a charmed life. He was born into one of Pittsburgh's most prominent and wealthy families in 1893. His grandfather was a railroad tycoon, coal baron, banker and philanthropist, and his father was a prominent businessman in Pittsburgh.

While attending Yale University, William developed a love of aviation, so much of one that he obtained a pilot's license. He would soon decide that college life was not for him, and in 1913, after completing his sophomore year, he dropped out to pursue flying full time. He convinced his father to buy him a hydroplane, which he used to roam the East Coast. In Newport, he gave passenger flights; in Palm Beach, he charged twenty dollars for a ride in his plane and ferried visitors over Lake Worth. Eventually, he found his way to New York City, where he was the first man to fly under all four bridges on the East River without touching the water.

By the spring of 1914, Alexander Thaw (who was known as Blair), William's younger brother, had invented an automatic stabilizer for heavy planes, and the brothers fitted it to William's hydroplane. In the summer of 1914, Blair Thaw's invention was chosen to represent the Aero Club of

America in a contest held in France. The brothers, along with their mother and sister, made the trip. However, before the winner could be decided, war erupted in Europe. Despite his mother's pleas to return with them to America, William decided to stay in France. He donated his hydroplane to the French government and attempted to become an aviator. He was turned down. The French barely had enough planes for their own men. Added to that, they were highly suspicious of young men willing to ignore their own government's neutrality to fight and die for the French cause. German spies and saboteurs could be anywhere. Undaunted, Thaw joined the war the only legal way he could. He, like hundreds of other young men, joined the French Foreign Legion as a private soldier. By his estimates, there were around 1,200 others from all over the world in his detachment.

Thaw, a natural leader, soon rose in the ranks, becoming a student-corporal while still in training, which gave him command over seven others, four cents a day instead of one and better shoes. He described his attempts to command his squad in a letter home, published in the *Yale Alumni Weekly*: "To add to my difficulties there were in it a chap from Flanders who spoke neither French nor English, [and] a Russian who didn't speak French…It took me two hours to get them to obey about twenty simple commands with any sort of precision. But it was a lot of fun."

By October 1914, Thaw and his battalion, which had been sent to Camp de Mailly in Chalons-sur-Marne, were ready for the front lines. By then, he had risen to the rank of first-class private. The front lines of "the greatest and probably last war" did not live up to Thaw's expectations. He soon found himself extremely bored. At the end of November he wrote, "War is wretched and uninteresting. Wish I were back dodging street cars on Broadway for excitement. Am that tired of being shot at!" His letters home tell of being cold and hungry and of long marches in which he was often a scout.

One of his more humorous stories occurred one night, when his unit was assured that a German attack was imminent. He and five others were the advanced guard, and went out about one hundred meters in front of the main line. He describes the theory behind it: "While the Germans were killing us off the others would be warned and have time to get ready. It was a peachy idea." However, instead of encountering thrilling gunfight, the members of the advanced guard instead stood in three inches of water for thirteen hours. Instead of Germans, cows wandered into the meadow across from them, scaring them half to death. Needless to say, it was not long before Thaw and a few of his American friends in the Legion wished to transfer to the French Aviation Service, which was not an easy task for Americans.

Thaw, however, was persistent. When he learned that an acquaintance of his, Lieutenant Brocard, was in charge of a French squadron, Thaw jumped at the chance to ask for his help. He hiked the roughly twenty miles to where Brocard was stationed to make his plea in person. The tactic worked, and by mid-December, he had been transferred to the French Aviation Service, along with fellow Americans James Bach and Bert Hall.

After a few weeks of observing the French fliers, it was time for the American pilots to show them what they could do. They began training on a Cauldron, a large aircraft, which Thaw, who was accustomed to flying a hydroplane, handled without difficulty. On December 23, 1914, he became the first American accepted in French Aviation Service. It was as an aviator that he would gain his fame, eventually earning a nickname from the French, the "American Eagle."

His rise in the French Aviation Service came quickly. In May 1915, he was awarded the war cross medal with a gold star and promoted to sergeant for his bravery. Under heavy German fire, he managed to signal from his airplane and direct the French retaliatory fire, helping to win the battle. In June, when he was sent on the reconnaissance mission over German lines, an anti-aircraft shell hit the tail of his plane, shattering it. Panicked and in danger of becoming a prisoner or worse, Thaw managed to land within the French lines. While on another reconnaissance mission, he managed to capture a photograph of a shell that had been fired at him as it exploded. He earned his third citation for bravery in August of that year, when he and another pilot had been assigned the work of locating and observing German batteries. A shell burst underneath his airplane, destroying a portion of the tail. He managed to pilot it through heavy fire and back across the French lines. On another scouting mission over enemy lines in 1916, Thaw, again under heavy fire, became separated from the rest of his escadrille. He took a machine gun ball in his arm, which fractured his left elbow. Adrenaline took over, and despite the loss of blood and the tremendous pain, Thaw managed to land his plane safely. He did not know what side of the lines he had landed on until he saw the blue uniforms of the French.

In December 1915, Thaw, along with fellow French pilots who were American citizens Norman Prince and Elliot Cowdin, returned to America for Christmas to much fanfare as his and his company's exploits were not unnoticed; however, because the United States was decidedly neutral, the men had to wear civilian clothes. That detail did not stop the press from covering them and, in many ways, treating them as ambassadors for the French cause. The *New York Times* and the Pittsburgh newspapers were especially obsessed with the returning aviators and greeted them as heroes. However, some pro-German newspapers called for their arrests.

The government turned a blind eye to those calls, though, and the men were allowed to return to France. By the time they returned to Paris in January 1916, they were determined to ask the French to form an American Escadrille in the flying corps. Their request was granted, and the Lafayette Escadrille was born. It was placed under the command of Captain Georges Thénault. The men were trained not only in reconnaissance but also on fighter planes. For the most part, the American pilots lived better than their French counterparts. This was due to the patronage of rich Americans sympathetic to French cause and proud of the young Americans who were serving.

Later in 1916, Thaw decided that their escadrille needed a mascot. He read in a newspaper that a Brazilian dentist was selling his lion cub for 500 francs. Thaw, along with a few of his friends, gained the capital to buy the lion, christened Whiskey. Shortly after purchasing the cub, Thaw attempted to take him on a passenger train, telling his fellow passengers and the conductor that he was an African dog. It might have worked, except the cub's roar gave the ruse away, and Thaw was forced to have a cage made for the lion so that it could ride in the luggage car. Eventually, Thaw would purchase another cub from the Paris zoo, naming it Soda. By all accounts, the lions were well behaved and quiet affectionate. However, when they grew to the size of large dogs, they began to make those outside the American escadrille nervous. The men were forced to give them up, and they lived out the rest of their lives in the Paris zoo. However, Soda and Whiskey never forgot their former owners. On a visit to the zoo, Thaw walked right up to their cage and stuck his hand through the bars to pet the two fully grown lions. To the surprise of the zookeepers and the reporter who witnessed the event, they rolled over for belly rubs.

Throughout the duration of the war, Thaw was cited several more times by the French for his bravery and his deeds. In addition to his other accomplishments, Thaw brought down at least five German airplanes, earning him the title of ace. Rising to the rank of lieutenant, he also earned the Croix de Guerre and the Medal of the Legion of Honor from France. In February 1918, the Lafayette Escadrille was transferred to the Americans, becoming the 103rd Pursuit Squadron of the American Air Services. The Americans made Thaw the commander of the squadron, promoting him to the rank of major. He eventually rose to the rank of lieutenant colonel and was awarded a Distinguished Service Cross with two citations by General Pershing.

William Thaw holding the lion cub Whiskey. *Courtesy of National Museum of the U.S. Air Force.*

After the war, Thaw returned to Pittsburgh, where he lived out the rest of his days. He entered into the insurance business and became a trustee of the Thaw Coke Trust. Eventually, Thaw settled down, marrying Marjorie Everts in the 1920s. However, he never lost his love of aviation or his sense of adventure. In September 1928, he decided to take part in an airplane race from New York City to Los Angeles, California. Along with Captain John P. Morris, Thaw flew a Lockerhead-Vega. Their attempt ended in near tragedy when a broken oil line caused them to crash at a farm outside Decatur, Illinois. There, they lay in their wreckage for over six hours, unable to move because of their wounds, until they were found the next morning. However, not one of the pilots that set out from New York that September made it all the way to Los Angeles.

Thaw's life was cut short in April 1934, when he died of pneumonia at the age of forty. He was survived by his widow and buried in his family plot at Allegheny Cemetery. His service was not forgotten by the French, however. In May 1934, they paid tribute to Thaw at Le Bourget field. A hollow square was formed by the Fifty-Fourth Squadron and reviewed by General Houcemont and Colonel Lahm, the air attaché of the United States Embassy. At the ceremony, Houcemont praised Thaw's skills as both an aviator and a leader. At the ceremony's conclusion, French planes dropped wreaths and flowers at the Lafayette Escadrille monument in Garches.

The Thaw family provided the war with two aviators, although William was the better known of the brothers. In December 1917, once America had entered the war, William's younger brother, Blair, followed in his footsteps. The eighteen-year-old had already been an aviator for two years when he joined the American Air Service. In the summer 1918, the younger Thaw was given command of a flying squadron. He was killed on August 18, 1918, when his plane engine developed trouble while in pursuit of enemies near the Paris front. His plane fell two thousand feet, struck telephone wires and collapsed upside down, killing him instantly. His passenger, Cord Meyer, and Blair's dog (who occupied a special seat in the plane) were injured but survived the crash.

Blair's body was taken to an evacuation hospital to be prepared for burial. His funeral was quite impressive, as described by the *New York Times*. The services were conducted by an Episcopal minister in a little chapel attached to a field hospital. Afterward, his coffin was placed on a truck, covered in flowers for the occasion, and slowly driven to the cemetery. Blair's squadron, William and their mother accompanied Blair on his final journey. He was interred with William's friend and member of the Lafayette Escadrille Raoul Lufberry.

William Thaw's grave marker in Allegheny Cemetery. *Courtesy of Andrew Williams and James Taggart.*

Although Blair Thaw's remains are in France, the Thaw family placed this marker in their family plot in Allegheny Cemetery to commemorate him. *Courtesy of Andrew Williams and James Taggart.*

Naturally, Blair Thaw was not the only Pittsburgher to die in the course of the war. Thomas Enright was born in Lawrenceville on May 8, 1887, to working-class Irish Catholic immigrants Ellen and John Enright. He was their seventh child and the first born on American soil. In his youth, he attended St. Mary's parochial school in Lawrenceville.

Perhaps out of a sense of adventure or an attempt to avoid the backbreaking life of his father and brothers, he followed his childhood friend Francis

DeLowery into the U.S. Armed Forces. DeLowery had joined the marines, Enright the army, becoming a member of the Twenty-sixth Cavalry in 1909 when he was twenty-two years old. Both men saw the world. Enright was in China and the Philippines. During the latter campaign, he earned the title of expert cavalryman.

DeLowery was killed during the U.S. occupation of Veracruz, Mexico, in 1914. Enright, who had been a part of the supporting infantry, wrote to his sister after learning of DeLowery's death, telling her that he was more anxious than ever to take on the Mexicans who had killed his friend.

Enright spent some time in Veracruz, and when his tour ran out in 1916, he reenlisted in the Sixteenth Infantry. Although not yet thirty years old, he was considered an old timer among the mostly new recruits. The Sixteenth Infantry would become part of the First Infantry and was among the first American troops in France. The infantry arrived in the summer of 1917. Enright's Company F, Sixteenth Infantry, was the first U.S. troops to see action on November 3, 1917, in what was to become known as the Bathlemont Raid.

At about 10:00 p.m. the night before, Company F relieved the French troops in the "quiet sector," protecting the city of Nancy, France. The German lines were about five hundred yards from the American trenches. The Americans had no way of knowing that the Germans were completely aware of their presence and their movements. They had been informed by a French deserter through a system of signals from the town of Bathlemont.

Enright was posted as a sentry along the lines, along with Private Merle D. Hay. The silence was broken about three o'clock in the morning by the sounds of German artillery. Corporal Frank Coffman later wrote that "the only thing that prevented our platoon from being entirely wiped out was the fact that our trenches were deep and the ground soft and muddy with no loose stones."

The Germans continued shelling for forty-five minutes, before, as Coffman describes, "the range was suddenly lifted in a half circle box barrage in our rear to prevent our support from coming up." During the shelling, the German troops had crawled under the gunshots right up to the American trenches without being spotted. They were ready to strike the moment the shelling stopped. About forty Americans found themselves face to face with over two hundred Germans. They were outnumbered ten to one as the Germans leapt over the parapet and into their trenches. The Americans had never experienced warfare like this before. Fighting the Germans in close quarters, they used their fists and rifle butts to attempt to repel the attack.

After about fifteen minutes the Germans retreated, taking eleven Americans prisoner, including two officers.

Three Americans—James B. Gresham from Evansville, Indiana; Merle D. Hay from Glidden, Iowa; and Thomas F. Enright—were dead. Enright, according to Coffman, was not found until the next morning. His comrades determined that he had been captured but had refused to leave with his German captors, putting up a fight instead. The Germans got the better of him in the end, cutting his throat from ear to ear. His chest was ripped open. There were twelve bayonet wounds on his body.

The first three American casualties were originally buried with military honors not far from where they died. The French general who was in command of Company F gave what was, by all accounts, a very moving speech. He reminded those gathered that these men gave their lives in a fight to save civilization, justice and honor from the forces of brutal barbarity. After relating their heroic deaths, he predicted that because of this, "their families, friends and fellow-citizens will be proud when they learn of their deaths." How right he was.

Word reached Pittsburgh of Enright's death by way of a telegram from Adjunct General McClain to Enright's sister Mary Irwin. He left behind another sister and two brothers. Mary was shocked when she received news of her brother's death. She hadn't heard from him since May and didn't even know he was in France. She managed, however, to respond to the *Gazette Times*, one of Pittsburgh's leading newspapers, which quoted her as saying, "While I grieve my brother's death I am proud to know that he died in defense of his country."

It was the *Gazette Times* that christened Enright a "martyr to democracy" when reporting his death on November 6, 1917. In death, the three men became something more than they could ever have imagined. They became symbols. They were all children of working-class parents. They were heroes and martyrs, and news of their deaths drove the sales of war bonds.

Mary asked for Enright's body to be returned to Pittsburgh, but her request was denied. It was the policy of the U.S. government, under recommendations from American general Pershing, that no bodies were to be sent home until after the war. Thomas Enright did not come back to Pittsburgh until 1921.

His body was accompanied by a member of Company F from the airport to the home of the Trunzers, his sister and brother-in-law. From there, it went to Soldiers and Sailors Memorial Hall in Oakland, where it lay in state. His casket was draped with an American flag and had an honor

This poster, used to raise money for the American war effort, depicts the first three American casualties of the war, including Pittsburgh native Thomas Enright. *Courtesy of the Library of Congress.*

Enright Court, located in the Pittsburgh neighborhood of East Liberty, is named for the Enright Theater, which previously occupied the location. The Enright Theater was named for Thomas Enright. *Courtesy of Andrew Williams.*

Enright's casket being carried out of Soldiers and Sailors Memorial Hall, 1921. *Courtesy of the Heinz History Center.*

Enright's funeral mass was held at St. Paul's Cathedral. A huge number of mourners paid tribute to the fallen hero. *Courtesy of the Heinz History Center.*

guard as thousands of mourners flocked past it. At around 10:00 a.m. on July 16, 1921, Pittsburghers observed a moment of silence for Enright. His casket was placed on a gun cassation by six pallbearers as "Nearer to My God Are Thee" played. His pallbearers were like him, graduates of St. Mary's and veterans of the war. Pittsburgh police escorted his body to St. Paul's Cathedral for his funeral. Also in attendance were veterans from every war, saluting the young hero. His funeral was celebrated by both the pastor from his home parish and Bishop Hugh C. Boyle. The cathedral was packed. Mayor Babcock had issued a proclamation that anyone who could attend the funeral should. In death, Enright belonged to the city in a way he never did in life. He was an outward symbol of Pittsburgh's pride, patriotism and wartime sacrifice. Enright's final journey ended in St. Mary's Cemetery in Lawrenceville.

CONCLUSION

America's entrance into World War I meant a great deal of sacrifices for Pittsburghers. Everyone, including children, was expected to aid in the war work (either through Red Cross work or through helping to raise funds for the war effort). Pittsburghers were expected to open their pocketbooks and buy Liberty Bonds (meeting government quotas was a source of civic pride and great celebration within the city). Food was rationed (sugar for example was needed to make explosives). The state even dictated what food items restaurants could serve (for example, in October 1918, rarebits, liver, bacon and any dish that contained two different kinds of meats were banned by the State Food Administrator). Reminders that every citizen had to do his part to defeat Germany were everywhere.

In addition to the other challenges that faced Pittsburghers, the worldwide Spanish influenza pandemic reached Pittsburgh in October 1918. The city had ample time to prepare and even sent nurses and doctors to Philadelphia and other infected areas when the outbreak was the heaviest. While the Pittsburgh Chapter of the Red Cross did its best to prepare for the worst-case scenario (including arranging for coffins to be made so that unburied bodies did not pile up like they had in Philadelphia), the city officials did not even follow the statewide ban on restricting gatherings. On September 29, despite military diagnoses of the flu in camps near the city, Mayor Babcock held a celebration in Forbes Field where forty thousand attended to bolster Liberty Loan sales. Schools throughout the county closed (including Pittsburgh's Catholic schools), but public schools remained open. Mr. Davis,

Young female munitions workers carrying the Allies' flags in a parade. Many patriotic parades were held throughout the war years in Pittsburgh. *Courtesy of the Heinz History Center.*

the city's public health leader, hoped that by monitoring the rates of sickness and death in children, he could keep tabs on conditions throughout the city. Public schools closed on October 24, twenty days after the state mandated that city doctors report cases of the flu. The city also allowed church services to continue (although Catholic churches and Jewish synagogues closed by their own accord) and permitted bars and other entertainment venues to remain open far longer than they should have been allowed. Even when the ban was in place, city bars and hotels openly ignored it with nothing more than a mild warning from city officials.

Pittsburgh also suffered a lack of nurses throughout the duration of the epidemic. Many had either gone to assist in other cities or had gone overseas. Local newspapers carried advertisements begging anyone with nursing experience to come forward to help. While several did, it was not enough to meet the growing need. At its height in mid-October, there was one new case of the flu every ninety seconds and one death every ten minutes. While the statewide ban on gathering ended in early November, the outbreak was not officially over until May 1919. By then 5,600 to 6,600 people had died from the flu (1 percent of Pittsburgh population). It was one of the hardest hit cities in the country.

Left: The view of downtown Pittsburgh from Mount Washington, 1919. *Courtesy of the Heinz History Center.*

Below: One of the many World War I monuments in Pittsburgh. It's located on a hillside in Schenley Park near the George Westinghouse monument. *Courtesy of Andrew Williams*.

Pittsburghers celebrating the announcement of the armistice in November 1918. *Courtesy of the Heinz History Center.*

Above: Homecoming parade for soldiers in Homestead, Pennsylvania. *Courtesy of the Heinz History Center.*

Left: This statue in front of Phipps Conservatory in the Pittsburgh neighborhood of Oakland commemorates the 450 members of the Allegheny County Medical Society who served in the war. *Courtesy of Andrew Williams and James Taggart.*

Opposite: This monument, located in the Pittsburgh neighborhood of Greenfield, is unique because it commemorates men and women from the neighborhood who served in both world wars. *Courtesy of Andrew Williams and James Taggart.*

Despite the pandemic, Pittsburgh's emotional ties to the war were so intense that it should come as no surprise that when the armistice was announced on November 11, a wave of pure happiness swept over the city. Hundreds and thousands of men and women filled the city streets, some weeping with joy. Impromptu parades formed in the streets (a more formal one was held that afternoon) as men and women streamed out of their places of business. Red, white and blue confetti filled the air, fluttering down from Pittsburgh's skyscrapers. At five minutes to noon, at the request of Mayor Edward Babcock, every streetcar, car and piece of machinery in Pittsburgh fell silent for five minutes to give people a moment to say a silent prayer of thanksgiving. From before dawn until long after dark, people celebrated in the streets. It did not matter that this was their second such celebration within a few days. Earlier that week, a mistaken report of peace had reached Pittsburgh and had received much the same reaction. All that mattered at that moment was the elation they felt. Pittsburghers' years of hard work and sacrifice had paid off in the form of an Allied victory.

It was the first of many postwar celebrations in Pittsburgh. Every time a unit of Pittsburgh's troops or nurses returned to the city, a parade was held for them. Pittsburghers turned out in droves to thank their brave sons and daughters for the sacrifices they had made. These parades were often

Left and below: The Pittsburgh neighborhood of Lawrenceville depicts what is perhaps its most famous resident, the doughboy in its newest logo. The statue's silhouette graces banners and garbage cans throughout the neighborhood. *Courtesy of Andrew Williams and James Taggart.*

Opposite: Pittsburgh's most famous World War I monument, the Lawrenceville Doughboy. *Courtesy of Andrew Williams and James Taggart.*

emotional for both those returning and those in attendance. It gave the city a chance to celebrate surviving the war.

In the years that followed, efforts were made to celebrate those who contributed to the war effort and commemorate those who had died. War monuments began to decorate the city as an everlasting tribute to the sacrifices Pittsburgh made. For the men, women and children who lived through it, World War I was the watershed moment that defined an entire generation. After all, they did not know that the Great Depression loomed. They did not know that in twenty years, Europe would be engulfed in another war, where Pittsburgh would again become the "Arsenal of the World." Today, while many of these monuments that were built have fallen into disrepair, others have become a part of the city's landscape and cultural memory, serving as a lasting symbol of the sacrifices that Pittsburghers made during the war.

SELECTED BIBLIOGRAPHY

ARCHIVAL SOURCES

Clark, John L. *The 351ˢᵗ Field Artillery History A.E.F. 1918*. Printed in 1942. World War I Clippings Collection. Pennsylvania Room, Carnegie Library, Oakland, PA.

Doran, Mary R. Scrapbook she made for her son, Sergeant Major J.G. Doran, 28th Division, 111th Infantry. 111th Infantry World War I box. Soldiers and Sailors Memorial Hall Archives, Pittsburgh, PA.

German Evangelical Protestant Smithfield Church Congregational History. Published in 1932. Smithfield United Church of Christ Archives.

Knights of St. George (September 1918, October 1918, November 1918). Newsletter. Diocese of Pittsburgh Archives, Pittsburgh, PA.

"A Service of Love and Sacred Memory for Mr. Donald C. Jefferson: August 14, 1895–April 17,1994." Heinz History Center Library and Archives, Pittsburgh, PA.

The Story of the Sixteenth Infantry in France: American Expeditionary Forces by the Regimental Chaplain. Frankfurt, Germany: Martin Flock, 1919. Thomas Enright folder. Soldiers and Sailors Memorial Hall Archives, Pittsburgh, PA.

ARTICLES

Altoona Mirror. "Knights Observing 100th Anniversary." May 3, 1918.

American Stationer. "Correspondence: Pittsburg." December 3, 1896.

Coffman, Frank. "And Then the War Began." *American Legion Weekly.* January 13, 1922.

Connors, Michael. "The Next Page: Finding Private Enright." *Pittsburgh Post-Gazette.* November 11, 2007.

Evening Public Ledger. "Philadelphia Guardsman Hurt on Coaster is Dead." July 7, 1917.

Gazette-Times. "Democracy Mothers to Care for Soldiers' Widows and Orphans." April 9, 1919.

———. "England's First Gas Mask Invented by Pittsburgher and Designed by his Wife." March 11, 1919.

———. "First Victim of Germans is Local Youth." November 5, 1917.

———. "Pittsburgh Viewed from the Outside: 'The Arsenal of the World and Figures Fall Short of Telling Story." Reprinted from *Christian Science Monitor.* February 28, 1918.

Gettysburg Times. "Held in Custody: Owner of Hotel Where Soldiers Ate." May 19, 1917.

Higgins, James. "'With Every Accompaniment of Ravage and Agony': Pittsburgh and the Influenza Epidemic of 1918–1919." *Pennsylvania Magazine of History and Biography* 134, no. 2 (July 2010): 263–86.

Iron Age. Advertisement for Carbon Steel on the cover of the July 24, 1919 issue.

———. "Pittsburgh in Turmoil." May 4, 1916.

———. "Strikes and Wages Advances: Pittsburgh Trouble Diminishing." May 11, 1916.

Kalson, Sally. "Cartoonist Draws, Fires a Blank with Pittsburgh Joke." *Pittsburgh Post-Gazette.* November 19, 2003.

Lee, Carmen J. "They Fought to Serve." *Pittsburgh Post-Gazette.* N.d.

Maier, Craig. "Local Catholics Play Decisive Role in 1918 Flu Pandemic" *Pittsburgh Catholic.* November 10, 2005.

McDonough, John J. "Our Duty." *Duquesne Monthly.* May 1917.

Milwaukee Journal. "Fall Kills Aviator, but Dog Escapes with Slight Limp." July 23, 1920

Nemmer, Edward. "The Anglo-American Peace Celebration." *Duquesne Monthly.* February 1915.

New York Times. "Americans Killed Must Lie in France Until War Ends." November 28, 1917.

————. "Assailed by a Mob." April 14, 1917.

————. "Bars Kreisler Concerts." November 7, 1917.

————. "Building of Shops Tied Up by Strike." September 18, 1917.

————. "Call Steel Plant Strike." September 20, 1917.

————. "C.F. Banning Freed from Internment." January 14, 1919.

————. "Cites Thaw Again for Courage in the Air." August 11, 1917.

————. "Closing Observed in All Large Cities." January 22, 1918.

————. "Cord Meyer Injured." August 30, 1918.

————. "Denies Secret War Work." July 4, 1917.

————. "$4,000,000 Fire Loss in a Munitions Plant: Machine Shop of Switch Signal Company in Pittsburgh Destroyed—Cause Unknown." February 11, 1917.

————. "France Honors Wm. Thaw." May 24, 1934.

————. "Fritz Kreisler Dies Here at 86: Violinist Composed 200 Works." January 30, 1962.

————. "Fritz Kreisler in a Statement of Great Frankness Tells of His Conduct in War." November 25, 1917.

————. "German Becoming Dead Tongue Here: Schools All Over America Banishing…" July 14, 1918

————. "Heat Cuts Steel Output." August 15, 1918.

————. "Kreisler Quits Concert Tour." November 26, 1917.

————. "Lieut. Blair Thaw Killed in France." August 23, 1918.

————. "Look for New Rise in Steel Wages." September 23, 1917.

————. "Nation-wide Plans to Avert Strikes" May 19, 1917.

————. "1916 Steel Output was 40,000,000 tons." January 7, 1917.

————. "Open 1917 with Rush for War Materials." January 14, 1917.

————. "Pershing's Men Fought Hand-to-Hand Against Overwhelming German Force, Battling Fiercely with Aid Cut Off." November 6, 1917.

————. "Pittsburgh Firemen Go on Strike." August 25, 1918.

————. "Pittsburgh May Bar Muck." November 6, 1917.

————. "Rich Propagandist Held in Pittsburgh." September 28, 1918.

————. "Steel Co. Subscribes $1,000,000." May 16, 1917.

————. "Steel Mills Near a Record Output." May 12, 1918.

————. "Steel Resources at Nation's Call." April 8, 1917.

————. "Thaw and Baer Cited." May 12, 1918.

————. "28 Killed by Gas Leak." November 10, 1918.

————. "Union Steel Strike." September 24, 1917.

————. "War Row Ends in Death." August 4, 1918.

———. "William Thaw 2D, Was Age 40, Dead." April 23, 1934.

Philadelphia Inquirer. "German Plot Hint Follows Poisoning of Soldier's Food." May 18, 1917.

———. "Hints at Sensation in Officer's Death." June 27, 1917.

———. "Lieutenant's Death Still a Mystery." July 7, 1917.

———. "Poisoned Guard's Host Is Arrested." May 19, 1917.

Pittsburgh Bulletin. "Sisterhood of War Mothers Organized in Pittsburgh." June 22, 1918.

Pittsburgh Catholic "Our Heroic Dead: First Americans Dead Are Buried While Enemies Shells Burst Close by." November 15, 1917.

Pittsburgh Chronicle Telegraph. "Army Officials in Conference." September 27, 1918.

———. "Doughboys Used Gas Protector Developed Here." Janurary 25, 1919.

———. "Polish Army Recruits Many from the City." October 2, 1918.

———. "Scientists Discovered Means to Defeat Fumes by Hun Army. Masks Good for War Only." January 25, 1919.

Pittsburgh Dispatch. "Tech Best War School in Country." September 6, 1918.

Pittsburgh Post-Gazette. "A Fact a Day about Pittsburgh: The Arsenal of the World." January 16, 1928.

Pittsburgh Press. "Alien Takes Beating: Patriot Gets Praised." April 17, 1917.

———. "All Quiet in Zone of Big Strike." April 23, 1916.

———. "Anti-War Advocate Jailed, Hearing Set." April 14, 1917.

———. "City is Ready to Answer Call, Says Dr. Kerr." April 1, 1917.

———. "Clashes Occur in Westinghouse Strike: East Pittsburgh Plant Is Scene of Disturbances." April 24, 1916.

———. "Enright's Body Lies in State at Hall." July 15, 1921.

———. "Expects to Solve Guard Poison Case." May 20, 1917.

———. "Forgotten Legion of War: Tom Enright's First to Fall." June 19, 1960.

———. "Forty Jones and Laughlin Strikers Go Back to Old Places." September 26, 1917.

———. "Great Throngs Pledge Fealty to 'Old Glory.'" April 1, 1917.

———. "Impressive Scene at Enright Funeral at Cathedral Yesterday." July 17, 1921.

———. "Impure Milk Is Blamed for Guard's Death." May 18, 1917.

———. "Mrs. Carl Miller Is Detained on Order of the Fire Marshal." May 21, 1917.

———. "National Guard May Be Called on Strike Duty." April 25, 1916.

———. "National Guard Quartered at Plant." May 5, 1916.

———. "Northside Patriotic Meeting." April 1, 1917.

———. "Probe Mystery of Poison that Killed Guard." May 17, 1917.

———. "R.J. McGrath's Stirring Speech." April 1, 1917.

———. "Senator Knox Urges People to Be True to the U.S." April 1, 1917.

———. "Shadyside Factory of Westinghouse If Closed: Government Sends Envoy to Probing Strike Here." April 27, 1916.

———. "Strike Cause of Clashes at Wilmerding, 10,000 March." April 26, 1916.

———. "Strikers Say They Will Not Accept Offer." September 24, 1917.

———. "Strike Zones Peaceful. Workers Only Showed Up to East Pittsburgh Plant." April 27, 1916.

———. "Strike Zone Policeman Complain of Deputies." April 28, 1916.

———. "13,000 Strike at Westinghouse Plant: Pickets Active and Deputies Are on the Scene." April 22, 1916.

———. "25 Years Ago This Was News." May 2, 1941.

———. "War Industry Badges Ready by September 1." August 18, 1918.

———. "War Move Not Surprising to Local Germans: Says Emperor and His Advisers Have Smarted Under Great Provocation for a Long Time." August 2, 1914.

———. "Wave of Patriotism Causes Flag Shortage." April 14, 1917.

———. "William Dilworth Surrenders Self After Man's Death." August 3, 1918.

———. "William Thaw is a Volunteer in the French Army." September 8, 1914.

Pittsburgh Sunday Leader. "Pastor and some of the Patriotic Members of the German Evangelical Protestant (Smithfield) Church. Be Patriotic, Dr. Voss Urges." August 4, 1918.

Pittsburgh Sun-Telegraph. "Children in School Must Aid War Work." November 11, 1918.

Semple, H.M. "Labor Disturbances in Pittsburgh Where Several Men Were Killed Early in May Investigated by the Members of the Industrial Board of the Department of Labor and Industry Report." *Monthly Bulletin of the Pennsylvania Department of Labor: A Bulletin of Information for the Public* 3, issue 7 (July 1916): 5–8.

Sunday Tribune. "Stubborn Fire in Pittsburgh." August 25, 1918.

Tarr, Joel A. "The Next Page: Carnegie Tech's On-Campus Gas Rig." *Pittsburgh Post-Gazette.* November 6, 2011.

Books

Alberts, Robert C. *Pitt: The Story of the University of Pittsburgh.* Pittsburgh, PA: University of Pittsburgh Press, 1986.

Allderdice, Ellen H. *An American Woman's Message*. Pittsburgh, PA: privately printed, 1917.

Anonymous. *Pittsburgh's Part in the World War: Souvenir Book of Stirring Scenes*. Pittsburgh, PA: Morris and Stauch, 1918.

Borkowski, Joseph A. *City of Pittsburgh's Park in the Formation of Polish Army— World War I 1917–1920*. Pittsburgh, PA: Central Council of Polish Organizations, 1956.

Brody, David. *Steelworkers in America: The Nonunion Era*. Cambridge, MA: Harvard University Press, 1960.

Campbell, Elizabeth A. *Audit of International Institute Material on Pittsburgh's Nationality Community*. Pittsburgh, PA: International Institute, 1928.

Chapter History Committee. *The Pittsburgh Chapter of the American Red Cross*. Pittsburgh, PA: Pittsburgh Printing Company, 1922.

Child, Clifton James. *The German-American in Politics 1914–1917*. Madison: University of Wisconsin Press, 1939; reprint, Arno Press and *New York Times*, 1970.

Cohn, Jan. *Improbable Fiction: The Life of Mary Roberts Rinehart*. Pittsburgh, PA: University of Pittsburgh Press, 1980.

Craughwell, Thomas J., and Edwin Kiester, Jr. *The Buck Stops Here: The Twenty-Eight Toughest Presidential Decisions and How They Changed History*. Minneapolis, MN: Fair Winds Press, 2010.

Dickerson, Dennis. *Out of the Crucible: Black Steelworkers in Western Pennsylvania 1875–1980*. Albany, NY: SUNY Press, 1986.

Doenecke, Justus D. *Nothing Less Than War: A New History of America's Entry into World War I*. Lexington: University of Kentucky Press, 2011.

Fenton, Edwin. *Carnegie Mellon 1900–2000: A Centennial History*. Pittsburgh, PA: Carnegie Mellon University Press, 2001.

Harper, Frank C. *Pittsburgh Today: Its Resources and People*. Volumes 1–2. New York: American Historical Society, Inc., 1931–32.

Hearings Before the Subcommittee on the Judiciary. U.S. Senate. 65th Congress. 2nd sess. S. 3529. February 23–April 13, 1918. Washington, D.C.: Washington Government Printing Office, 1918.

Hough, Emerson. *The Web*. Chicago: Reilly and Lee Company, 1919.

Johnson, Charles Thomas. *Culture at Twilight: The National German-American Alliance 1901–1918*. New York: Peter Lang, 1999.

McCormick, Charles H. *Seeing Reds: Federal Surveillance of Radicals in the Pittsburgh Mill District, 1917–1921*. Pittsburgh, PA: University of Pittsburgh Press, 1997.

Morse, Edwin W. *America in the War: The Vanguard of American Volunteers in the Fighting Lines and in Humanitarian Service August 1914–April 1917*. New York: Charles Scribner's Sons, 1919.

Rishel, Joseph F. *"The Spirit That Gives Life": The History of Duquesne University, 1878–1996.* Pittsburgh, PA: Duquesne University Press, 1997.

Rook, Charles Alexander, ed. *Western Pennsylvanians: A Work for Newspaper and Library Reference.* Pittsburgh: Western Pennsylvania Biographic Association, 1923.

Shaughnessy, Michael. *German Pittsburgh.* Chicago: Arcadia Publishing, 2007.

Thenault, Captain Georges. *The Story of the Lafayette Escadrille Told by Iits Commander.* Translated by Walter Duranty. Boston, MA: Small Maynard and Company, 1921.

Trotter, Joe William Jr., and Eric Ledell Smith. *African Americans in Pennsylvania.* University Park: Pennsylvania State University Press, 1997.

Warren, Wilson J. *The Greater Beneficial Union of Pittsburgh: The Changing Dimensionsof a Fraternal Enterprise, 1892–1992.* Company history published by the Greater Beneficial Union.

Workers of the Writers' Program of the Works Project Administration in the Commonwealth of Pennsylvania. *The Story of Old Allegheny City.* Pittsburgh, PA: Allegheny County Centennial Committee, 1941.

Papers/Theses

Cronin, Michael Francis. "A Survey of Pro-German Propaganda Printed in the Leading Newspapersof Pittsburgh Pennsylvania During 1914–1915." Master's thesis, Duquesne University, 1948.

Miller, Cheryl Lynn. "Der Volksblatt und Freiheits Freund: Loyalties of German-Americans in Pittsburgh During World War I." Written as part of a tutorial in German at Chatham College, April 25, 1985.

Websites

Glasco, Laurence. "Double Burden: The Black Experience." http://www.angelfire.com/jazz/larryglasco/H1669/Burden.pdf (accessed March 20, 2013).

History Channel. "This Day in History: June 28, 1914: Archduke Franz Ferdinand assassinated." http://www.history.com/this-day-in-history/archduke-franz-ferdinand-assassinated (accessed January 3, 2013).

Jones, Marian Moser. "The American Red Cross and Local Response to the 1918 Influenza Pandemic: A Four-City Case Study." http://www.ncbi.nlm.nih.gov/pmc/articles/PMC2862338/ (accessed May 1, 2013).

National Public Radio (NPR). "The Great Migration: The African American Exodus North." http://www.npr.org/templates/story/story.php?storyId=129827444 (accessed March 21, 2013).

Public Broadcasting System (PBS). "Meet Andrew Carnegie: Welcome to Pittsburgh" http://www.pbs.org/wgbh/amex/carnegie/sfeature/meet_pittsburg.html (accessed April 10, 2013).

Rejali, Darius. "Electricity: The Global History of a Torture Technology." http://academic.reed.edu/poli_sci/faculty/rejali/articles/History_of_Electric_Torture.html (accessed February 15, 2013).

Tabery, James, Charles W. Mackett III, and the UPMC Pandemic Influenza Task Force's Triage Review Board. http://www.canprep.ca/library/EthicsOfTriageInPandemic.pdf (accessed May 1, 2013).

Thirteen. "Fritz Kreisler." http://www.thirteen.org/publicarts/violin/kreisler.html (accessed March 14, 2013).

University of Pittsburgh, Slovak Studies Program. "Pittsburgh Agreement." http://www.pitt.edu/~votruba/qsonhist/pittsburghagreement.html (accessed June 1, 2013).

Western Pennsylvania Brownfields Center. "Neville Island." http://www.cmu.edu/steinbrenner/brownfields/Case%20Studies/pdf/neville%20island.pdf (accessed April 10, 2013).

Wordnet. "Rifle Grenade." http://wordnetweb.princeton.edu/perl/webwn?s=rifle%20grenade. (accessed January 21, 2013).

"WWI Housing: Neville Island" http://web.mit.edu/ebj/www/ww1/NevilleIsland.html (accessed April 10, 2013).

INDEX